I KNOW
ABSOLUTELY
NOTHING
A B O U T™
SNOWBOARDING

I KNOW
ABSOLUTELY
NOTHING
A B O U T™
SNOWBOARDING

A New Snowboarder's Guide
to the Sport's History,
Equipment, Apparel, Etiquette,
Safety, and Language

Steve Eubanks and Mark Fawcett

Rutledge Hill Press
Nashville, Tennessee

Published in Nashville, Tennessee, by Rutledge Hill Press, 211 Seventh Avenue North, Nashville, Tennessee 37219.

Distributed in Canada by H. B. Fenn & Company, Ltd., 34 Nixon Road, Bolton, Ontario L7E 1W2.

Distributed in Australia by The Five Mile Press Pty., Ltd., 22 Summit Road, Noble Park, Victoria 3174.

Distributed in New Zealand by Tandem Press, 2 Rugby Road, Birkenhead, Auckland 10.

Distributed in the United Kingdom by Verulam Publishing, Ltd., 152a Park Street Lane, Park Street, St. Albans, Hertfordshire AL2 2AU.

Typography by D&T/Bailey Typesetting, Inc., Nashville, Tennessee.

Inside illustrations by David Alden.

Cover photo of snowboarder Sherry Newstead by permission of Scott Serifas Photo.

Library of Congress Cataloging-in-Publication Data

Eubanks, Steve, 1962–
    I know absolutely nothing about snowboarding : a new snowboarder's guide to the sport's history, equipment, apparel, etiquette, safety, and the language / Steve Eubanks and Mark Fawcett.
        p.   cm.
    ISBN 1-55853-546-2 (pb)
    1. Snowboarding.   I. Fawcett, Mark, 1972–   .   II. Title.
GV857.S57E83   1997
796.9—dc21   97-35300
                                                    CIP

Printed in the United States of America

1   2   3   4   5   6   7   8   9—00 99 98 97

To my sons, James, Jonathan, Andrew, Aaron and Ben Eubanks—future snowboarders all.

—Steve Eubanks

To all those professional riders and skiers who have lost their lives in pursuit of their dreams, this is for you.

—Mark Fawcett

CONTENTS

Acknowledgments

Two of the greatest things about creating a book are developing friendships and meeting people along the way. We want to thank Brian Albert of Advantage International for bringing us together as co-authors and for spearheading this project from the beginning. Brian planted the seed for what we now believe is a great book and we know is a great friendship. To Mike Towle, a tireless editor and patient friend, we offer our most sincere thanks. Thanks also to publisher Larry Stone for his belief and devotion to this and all the *I Know Absolutely Nothing About*™ books.

We owe a world of thanks to 1995 World Extreme Snowboard Champion Steve Klassen, along with Jeff Smith and the entire staff at the Wave Rave Snowboard Shop, for providing us with tons of information and patiently answering all of our questions. Thanks also to the members of the Cross M Snowboard Team and the Fila 24:7 team for spending the time and making the effort to help. Without these people's efforts, this book would not be a reality.

Once again, immeasurable thanks go to our illustrator David Alden, who consistently amazes us with some of the most creative and memorable "notes" ever put on paper.

And, as always, we want to thank Debbie Eubanks and Sky Rondenet for supporting us in all our endeavors and for making life better every day.

INTRODUCTION

As is the case for many men who have left their twenties to discover the joys of puttering in a garage and sitting in a favorite chair, the thought of taking up a new sport, especially a sport with as militant a reputation as snowboarding, was as foreign to me as flying on the space shuttle. It didn't take long to discover that such narrow-minded thinking is silly.

During my first day on the mountain, I learned that all my preconceived notions about snowboarding were wrong. Those who think the sport is reserved for the young and radical are missing out on an exhilarating experience with life-changing potential. Nothing is more exciting than standing on top of a snow-covered peak and gazing out at the whitest landscape and bluest sky you've ever seen. The sense of freedom and permission that one experiences while shredding fresh powder transcends the realm of sport and recreation and truly touches the rider's soul. For those who haven't experienced it, there's nothing like it on earth.

I was lucky enough to take up the sport in the company of one of the world's top-ranked competitors, to whom I owe a great indebtedness. Mark Fawcett is not just a world-class athlete, he is a world-class person, someone who made learning fun without ever making me feel inferior (which I clearly was) or foolish. Mark and I hope to accomplish the same with you.

Before you can experience the wonders of snow-boarding, you must know enough to get started. Like all the *I Know Absolutely Nothing About*™ titles, this book is a fun, fast, and easy-to-understand guide to, in this case, the world's fastest-growing alpine winter sport. The story is designed to teach as well as entertain. As such, we've taken certain liberties with the intelligence of our main character. No one could be quite as ignorant as our Adam, nor are you likely to experience the kind of patient, sycophantic service Adam receives on his trek through the world of snowboarding. Snowboarding people are friendly (moreso than most sports since everyone who rides works hard to overcome the sport's less-than-mainstream image) but they are also very busy. You are not likely to find anyone who will spend the kind of time with you that our character receives. That's why we wrote the book: Adam asks all the potentially embarrassing questions. All you have to do is read.

So, sit back (in your favorite chair), suspend disbelief, and enter a culture that's bound to grab you, hold you, and make you a believer. Join us in the wonderful, fast, fun world of snowboarding.

—Steve Eubanks

Foreword

Having grown up competing on a snowboard, I will be the first to admit that those of us in the sport can easily lose touch with those folks who know absolutely nothing about snowboarding. That's why putting this book together was one of the most exhilarating experiences of my career, indeed my life.

Helping others who are interested in our sport is the goal of all professional snowboarders. I've won more than thirty professional titles, but no victory can match the feeling you get when you see the face of a new rider who has completed his or her first run. Hopefully, this book will be the first step in getting more people involved in snowboarding and in expanding the sport to new areas of the world.

On behalf of all the professionals who love the sport and everything it stands for, I want to welcome you to a lifestyle you're bound to love forever. Welcome to snowboarding.

—Mark Fawcett

Steve Eubanks is an outdoors enthusiast whose previously co-authored *I Know Absolutely Nothing About*™ books are about golf, skiing, and tennis. Eubanks also is the author of *Augusta: Home of the Masters Tournament* as well as three novels. He lives in Huntsville, Alabama.

Mark Fawcett is a veteran snowboarder and winner of numerous world championships. He took first place in seven international giant-slalom events during the 1996–97 season, and he's expected to contend for a medal at the 1998 Winter Olympics in Japan. Fawcett lives in Hood River, Oregon.

I KNOW
ABSOLUTELY
NOTHING
A B O U T ™
SNOWBOARDING

One

Snow Bored

Adam's parents and two siblings describe him as restless. No doubt he is active, and with his twenty-seventh birthday coming up in less than a month, he shows no signs of slowing down. Adam runs, body surfs, dives—both sky and scuba—and plays league rugby; but since taking his new job, he's been unable to do any of that stuff. Not that he doesn't still love the excitement: It's just that with the new job came a new location—inland, near snow-covered mountains.

"People would kill to live where you live," Adam's friends tell him, and they are right. With an office window that reveals snow-capped peaks and an apartment that gives new meaning to the term *high-rise,* Adam is the envy of all his old beach buds. It's just that he misses the rush of being the first swimmer to hit the morning beach break or freefalling toward earth at alarming speeds or mingling with undersea life as he explores an old shipwreck.

Adam also has an infatuation that goes beyond the outdoors. Her name is Leta, like him an account executive at his new firm. Her office is two doors down from his, and even though Adam has made subtle overtures toward Leta, as far as he can figure out the interest isn't mutual. Oh yeah, she offers an obligatory "Good morning" every day as he passes her at the coffee machine, but she doesn't seem to notice that his eyes linger a little too long or that his voice goes up an octave when he returns her daily greeting. He wants to ask her out. But even though he's fearless in almost everything else, when it comes to dating, Adam lacks nerve.

This morning is no different. Adam's palms begin to sweat as he closes two files, gets up from behind his desk, and walks out for the morning ritual of making small talk with Leta. Two deep breaths and he tells himself today is going to be *the* day. What's the worst that could happen? If she says no, laughs, comes up with some excuse, or, even worse, sighs and says something lame like "Oh, how sweet," he will get the hint. Besides, at some point she's going to realize that he doesn't like coffee.

"Morning, Adam."

He looks up and sees Leta standing before him, coffee cup in hand. She is wearing a stylish kiwi-green suit that flatters her athletic figure. As her smile glows under the florescent office lighting, Adam is struck by another thought: *She is too beautiful to go out with me.*

"Adam?"

"Oh, good morning," he says.

"How was your weekend?"

He hesitates. This is the first time she's ever asked about his weekend. "Pretty lame, I'm afraid," he admits. "I haven't been able to get into a routine yet." It's hard to explain to someone how much you miss skydiving when most people can't relate to jumping out of an airplane. The conversation renews his courage, however, and he opens his mouth to ask Leta out to dinner, only to be interrupted.

"Hi, Leta. Hi, Adam."

It's Chris, one of the young turks from the creative department. Although Chris's timing is bad, Adam has come to like Chris in the short time they've known each other. As usual, Chris is wearing jeans and an open flannel work shirt over a bright rose cotton tee. Part of Adam's affinity for twenty-one-year-old Chris is his envy of the younger man's laid-back sense of style. Even the renegades at Adam's old job weren't really unique in their rebellion. They dressed and acted cutting edge, but they were all alike, as if they were taking cues from the *Radical Gen-X Handbook*. Chris, on the other hand, is genuine, all the way down to his sandal-clad, sockless feet.

"Hi, Chris," Leta responds.

"Good morning," Adam adds.

"Hey, Leta, you need to come with us in a couple of weeks," Chris says. "There's a rad new terrain park opening near the half pipe. I hear they've got some killer table tops."

"Oh yeah?"

Adam listens but says nothing. He has no clue why Leta would be interested in some park with tables, so he decides to eavesdrop while Chris fills her in.

"Yeah. You know I just mounted this new step-in binding set-up this weekend. I was railing through the old park. At one point, I hit two banks, floated straight into the gap jump, and landed my first back-side 540. I was stoked."

Adam is captivated yet confused. This sounds exciting, whatever it is.

"Great," Leta says. "How did the step-ins respond?"

"Really well," Chris answers. "I was surprised by just how well they did respond, in fact. A couple of times I expected to feel some chatter, but it turned out to be really smooth."

"That's great to hear," Leta says. "I was thinking about changing out my sky-backs. Did Josh go with you?"

Leta's obvious familiarity with Chris's bizarre language is compelling Adam to pay even closer attention. This is one conversation that he's not going to let slide by.

"No," Chris replies. "You didn't hear?"

"Hear what?" she asks.

"He's out for a while. There was some sick powder on the north shoot last week, and he got sluffed out. I saw him take some rad endo's."

"Is he all right?" she presses.

Adam still doesn't know what they're talking about, but he assumes getting "sluffed out" and "taking some rad endo's" is not good.

"Yeah, he's fine. He'll probably go with us to the new park in a couple of weeks. Can we count you in?"

"Sure," Leta answers. "I'm stoked for some big air, as long as I don't flatbottom on those table tops. I still have to come in here on Monday."

Adam still has no clue as to what's going on, but it's getting more intriguing by the minute. He figures that a "flatbottom on a table top" must be code for something, but he can't imagine what it could be, and he's not about to open his mouth and embarrass himself with his ignorance.

"So, how about you, Adam?" Chris inquires. "Do you ride?"

Adam's blank expression answers for him: *Ride what?*

"Have you ever snowboarded?" Chris continues.

Snowboarding. *Of course.* What else would a guy like Chris do in a town like this?

"No," Adam responds. "In fact, I know absolutely nothing about snowboarding."

"You want to learn?" Leta asks.

Adam would have said yes had she asked him to climb Mount Everest in his underwear. "Sure. I've been looking for something new to take on."

"Great," Chris exclaims. He reaches into his wallet, pulls out a tattered business card, and hands it to Adam. "The guy that owns this shop is a friend of mine. Give him a call. He can set you up with every-thing you need."

Adam reads the card: Wild Ride Snowboard Shop.

"So, are you going to try out the new park with us?" Leta asks.

"I don't know," Adam says, still looking at the card and wondering what he's committing to. "I guess I should check out this shop first . . . maybe get a lesson or something."

"The park won't be ready for another couple of weeks," Chris explains. "You'll be jibbing by then."

"Sure, I guess," says Adam, who's suddenly starting to feel the rush he's been missing since taking this job. Snowboarding could be just what he needs to re-energize himself.

"Great," Leta pronounces. "You're going to love it. Snowboarding is something you can really get passion-ate about."

That seals it for Adam: If Leta is this passionate about snowboarding, then he'll love it as well. He says his good-byes and retreats to his office to call the Wild Ride Snowboarding Shop.

"Wild Ride, this is Tara. Can I help you?" a friendly female voice answers.

"Hi, Tara. I hope you can help me. My name's Adam, and a coworker of mine gave me your card. I'm not from the area, and I've never been on a snowboard. I've never even skied—"

"Have you surfed?" she interrupts.

"A couple of times. Body surfing and parasailing are more my thing."

"All right, an extremist! Have you ever skateboarded?"

"No, but I ice skate."

"Perfect. When can you come in?"

Adam checks his work schedule and sees that even with a full day today, he can work late on the Oracle proposal and take some time tomorrow. "How about in the morning?" he asks.

"Super. I get in at eight. Meet me here?"

"I'll see you at eight." Adam hangs up and stares at the business card again. This really is going to be a wild ride.

Two

Now Boarding

The first thing Adam notices is the music. Before reaching the front door of the Wild Ride Snowboarding Shop, Adam hears a familiar guitar riff blaring over a pair of outdoor speakers. It's a Smashing Pumpkins tune—young, radical, and appropriate for the world in to which he is about to enter. As Billy Corgan's voice fills his ears, Adam pulls open the large oak door and steps inside.

It's bigger than he had expected. His preconceived idea of a snowboard shop was a seedy, hole-in-the wall store with a concrete floor and a tattooed teenager sitting in a dark corner. This place, however, is brightly lit, clean, and carpeted. Adam is struck by the rows of boards perched on end near the front door. At first glance they look like surfboards, but as he gets closer he's amazed by the different sizes, shapes, and exotic colors. These boards bear some of the features of trick water skis, although it's tough to say they perfectly resemble anything.

"Welcome to Wild Ride!"

Adam looks up to see an attractive young woman with shoulder-length brown hair and a natural, earthy smile walking toward him. Her long, sweeping gait screams *athlete*.

"I'm Tara Earhart," she greets Adam, firmly shaking his hand.

"Hi, Tara, I'm Adam. I recognize your voice from our phone call yesterday."

"Oh yeah. You're the guy who knows absolutely nothing about snowboarding."

"Yep, that's me. This wouldn't be a big deal, except I've committed to go snowboarding with some friends in a couple of weeks."

"It's called riding," Tara clarifies. "Nothing tips off your inexperience quicker than saying you're going snowboarding. You ride a snowboard, and the act of snowboarding is usually called riding. You're going to love it. There's nothing like linking your first carved turns. Before you know it, you're riding down the slopes and drinking in one of the greatest feelings in the world. Believe me, snowboarding is as fun as it looks."

Adam hears words like *linking* and *carving* and realizes this is going to require more than just his paying close attention. Fortunately, he carries a notepad with him for those inconvenient moments when inspiration usually strikes. Lately, he's been uninspired—the pages are blank. After Adam checks every pocket and fumbles for an awkward moment, Tara hands him a pen.

"So, how did snowboarding get started?" Adam begins. "I mean, did some surfer make a wrong turn and end up on the top of a mountain?"

Tara smiles. "That's not far from wrong. The guy credited with inventing snowboarding is American surfer Sherman Poppen. In the 1960s he came up with a contraption that was an inexpensive combination of surfboard, skateboard, and water ski. Poppen called his new invention the SNURFER, for snow-surfer. Snurfing was fun, but hairy. The boards had no bindings, which meant your feet weren't attached. You just stood on the snurfers in regular boots and tried to maneuver down the hill with a rope fastened to the front of the board."

"Like the tow-rope used in water skiing?" Adam asks.

"More like the reigns on a Brahma bull," Tara answers. "We're not talking about a lot of control here. Snurfing was for the truly extreme, but it provided the genesis for today's snowboarding. In fact, two people on opposite sides of the United States took Poppen's snurfer idea and modified it into what we now know as the modern snowboard. The first was a radical snurfer-freak named Jake Burton Carpenter, from Vermont. Jake took his cue from the Vermont skiers and attached crude bindings to his snurfer, eliminating the need for the rope.

"Out in California a guy named Tom Sims, who just happened to be a world-champion skateboarder, modified the snurfer to incorporate some of the design features of an oversized skateboard. As it caught on, more innovations came, and by the mid-1980s, snowboarders were rocking the world. Jake and Tom kept improving their designs, and now they operate two of the most successful snowboard companies in the world: Burton and Sims."

Adam writes all this down and keys in on something Tara said. "You said snurfing was for the truly extreme, but I've always had the impression that snowboarding is an extreme sport. Wrong impression?"

"Today it is," she asserts. "Snowboarding is only about thirty years old, so you've got to figure that the first people to try it were, like, real edgy, innovative, and, yeah, extreme types. Those guys loved pushing the edge, and there are still a lot of riders out there who fit that same mold. Freeriding came out of that genre of snowboarding, but today you've got kids, families, retirees—all kinds of different people taking it up. It's graceful, it's free-flowing, and it has a sort of pared-down simplicity that you don't find in any other winter sport. That's what makes it so popular. You know, for a lot of years, the majority of resorts wouldn't allow snowboards because of that radical image you're talking about. Now they do whatever they can to attract riders. Without snowboarding, many resorts would be out of business."

Adam nods and checks his notes. "What's freeriding?" he asks.

"Good question," she acknowledges with a smile. "The three different styles of snowboarding are:

- ALPINE CARVING, which is, in essence, carving turns down the mountain without worrying

about tricks or style. Slalom racing is considered alpine carving. At the other end of the spectrum you have . . .

- FREESTYLE, which is that radical extreme element you were just asking about. When you see guys catching big air, doing flips, grabs, spins— all that sort of stuff—that's freestyle. Somewhere in between alpine carving and freestyle is a style called . . .

- FREERIDE, which isn't strictly downhill carving, but it isn't strictly jumps and tricks, either. Freeriding is the most popular style because it allows a little of everything. It's what you'll be doing when you first start, and it might be the style you stick with forever."

Adam looks up. "Wait a second. What the heck are big air, grabs, spins, and slaloms? The only word in there I recognized was flips, and I won't be doing any flips, not intentionally anyway."

Tara laughs. She explains that within the differing styles of snowboarding there are various characteristics that separate one style of riding from another. Alpine carving, for example, is a racing style, while freestyle is more of an acrobatic style. Freeriding combines the two and encourages riders to experience different terrains while carving, jumping, and enjoying the mountain in its totality.

"CATCHING AIR is when you get airborne," Tara says. "Big air is when you get high in the air. It's snowboarding's equivalent to hang-time. Spins are just that, spinning around while in the air. When you're talking about spins, you usually do it in terms of the degrees of rotation the rider spins. A 180 is when the rider spins one-half rotation—180 degrees—which isn't that difficult, relatively speaking. A 360 means 360 degrees—one full rotation. A 720 is two rotations: The rider catches big air (gets airborne) and makes two complete spins before landing."

"Sort of like a double axle in figure skating," Adam observes.

"Good analogy," Tara agrees. "A flip is a somersault where the rider goes end over end, and that shouldn't be confused with a spin. Also, when catching air you'll hear riders refer to tail grabs, nose grabs, and various other grabs. Those are, as the names imply, different ways the rider grabs the board. Another word you'll hear sometimes is FAKIE, or SWITCH-STANCE, which means backward. Any time the snowboard is traveling backward it's called fakie."

She looks at Adam and sees she might be losing him again.

"Okay, so you're riding, and you hear someone say he just landed a 360 tail-grab fakie. What happened?"

Adam reviews his notes for a second before answering. "It sounds like he was riding backward and caught air, then spun one full rotation while grabbing his board. He landed fakie, which means the back of the board was leading."

"Excellent," Tara says. "Now, as for your question about slaloms, each discipline has its own unique competitions." Tara lists the alpine carving competitions as:

- SLALOM
- DUAL SLALOM
- GIANT SLALOM
- SUPER G

These are races along courses where the rider must navigate through gates set at various points along a slope. The dual slalom is also a race through gates, but rather than racing against a clock, riders actually race side-by-side against each other on two identical courses.

"What are gates?" Adam asks, envisioning a fence or a swinging door of some kind.

"GATES are triangular panels set up along the slope that the rider must go around on his or her way down the run. The different types of slaloms are based on the distance between gates. On slalom courses, the gates are pretty close together, so riders have to make tight, accurate turns. Giant slalom and super-G courses are set up with the gates farther apart, so speed through the turns becomes a much bigger deal."

Adam jots all this down before asking his next question. "So, what are freestyle and freeride competitions?"

"Freeride competitions include some of the rad runs you've probably seen on television. In fact, the WORLD EXTREME CHAMPIONSHIP is considered a freeride event. Riders pick out some of the sickest runs you've ever seen and take the most extreme lines they can find, all the way down the mountain. They're judged on difficulty, style, and completion. Freestyle is also judged on things like style, transition,

DIFFERENT RIDES FOR DIFFERENT FOLKS

FREERIDER

CARVER

RACER

FREESTYLER

rotation, and landing. These events include the half pipe and the slopestyle. Now, I don't expect you to remember or even understand most of these, but it's good to understand that there are competitions within each style of snowboarding, some judged and some put on a clock, just like speed skating and figure skating."

Adam gives her an understanding nod. "So, who's the best?" he wants to know.

"I'm sorry?" she says, not completely understanding what it is Adam is attempting to ask.

"If there are all these competitions, there have to be winners and losers. Who's the world's number-one rider?"

"Well, that depends," Tara says, and she laughs at how noncommittal her answer sounds. "There have been lots of greats over the years, and it's tough to compare one discipline with another, just like it's tough to compare one era with another. Snowboard technology, for example, is so much better now than just five or ten years ago that it's almost impossible to compare riders from the two eras. Terje Haakenson from Norway, for example, is probably the best athlete ever to put on a snowboard. He's a three-time world champion, but then Bertrand Denerveau from Switzerland has won four world championships in the all-around division. Is Haakenson better than Denerveau? It depends on whom you ask."

Tara then gives Adam a rundown of her personal picks for riders to remember. They include:

RACING COMPETITIONS INCLUDE
SLALOM. GIANT SLALOM. DUAL SLALOM.
AND SUPER G.
FREERIDE COMPETITIONS INCLUDE THE
WORLD EXTREME CHAMPIONSHIP.

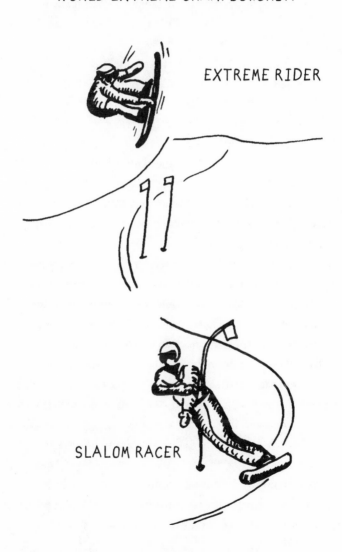

EXTREME RIDER

SLALOM RACER

- Terry Kidwell, from California, the originator of the freestyle discipline;
- Craig Kelly, from Washington, a five-time world champion;
- Michelle Taggart, from Oregon, a former world champion considered by many to be the world's best overall female rider;
- Tom Burt, "the King of Extreme";
- Jeff Brushie, a groundbreaking freestyler and former world champion;
- and Germany's Peter Bauer, considered the sport's original carver.

Adam writes down all the names before looking up again.

"That's quite a list," Adam remarks. "I won't get anywhere near these guys, but it's good to know whom to emulate."

Tara laughs at this. "Before you can challenge anybody, we've got to get you suited up." She steps around him and yells to someone in the back of the store. A moment later a tall man with wavy brown hair and the rugged face of an outdoorsman steps out from behind a counter. "Adam, this is Stan Klassen, equipment expert," Tara says. "Stan, this is Adam, a new rider who has chosen our shop as his first stop to a newfound life as a rider."

Adam extends his hand and Stan shakes it enthusiastically. "Tara's not being totally honest," Adam says. "I know absolutely nothing about snowboarding, and I've promised some friends I'd go riding with them in a couple of weeks. Actually, one friend

. . . a coworker . . . anyway, I don't want to disap-
point her."

Tara and Stan chuckle at this new revelation.
"Come this way, my friend. It's time you learned a
little about what you're going to be riding," Stan says.

Three

On-Board Basics

Stan picks up one of the boards from the front display and begins his lecture. "There are four different types of snowboards that come in hundreds of sizes, flexes, and construction styles. Even with all the variations, however, there are a few things that remain universal no matter what kind of board you have."

Stan places the rear of the board on the floor and turns it so the board is facing Adam. "The top of the board," he explains, pointing to the end that's in the air, "is known as the NOSE. If you think about going straight downhill on this board, which, by the way, isn't cool, the nose of the board is in front of you. The back end of the board," he points to the end near the floor, "is called the TAIL."

Adam nods and draws a board, labeling the parts.

Stan continues, "The area in the center is called the WAIST. Note how snowboards have a subtle hourglass shape."

Adam peers at the board and sees how the waist is narrower than the nose and tail, so with a little imagination he gets the idea.

"That narrowing effect you see is called SIDECUT," Stan goes on. "Sidecut helps turning. With the same amount of motion, a board with more sidecut will turn quicker than one with less sidecut. It's sort of like power steering. Some boards have a very pronounced sidecut; some have very little sidecut—it depends on what the board is designed to do."

Stan turns the board sideways so that Adam is looking at its thin, curved profile. "The corners of the board, where the top, bottom, and sides meet, are called the EDGES. The actual side of the board is called the SIDEWALL, but you won't hear that term as much as you will hear people discussing the edge or edges of the board.

"Without getting too technical, you control your board by making turns, and you turn your board by placing it on edge. Imagine for a second that you're flying in an airplane. When the airplane turns left, it banks, or rolls, to the left. The left wing dips and the plane leans into the turn. When it turns right, the plane banks right."

Adam gives an understanding nod.

"Okay, now imagine a snowboard going down a hill. In order to turn that board, you have to bank it, or place the board on edge, just like an airplane." He wags the board back and forth to simulate movement from one edge to the other. "It's very important that you check the edges of any board you're considering."

TYPES OF SNOWBOARDS
AND SNOWBOARDERS

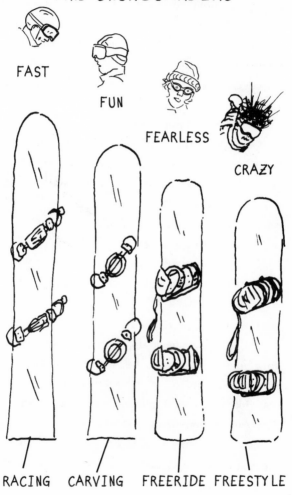

FAST

FUN

FEARLESS

CRAZY

RACING   CARVING   FREERIDE FREESTYLE

"Check them for what?" Adam queries.

"Nicks, abrasions—anything that might inhibit a smooth glide along the snow." Stan runs the back of his index finger along the edge of the board. He further explains that you should be able to run your fingernail along the edge of the board without feeling any rough abrasions. If the surface is rough, it will feel rough on the snow. Make it a point to always check the edges, which is especially critical if you're renting a board.

"Is it better to rent than buy?" Adam asks.

"As a beginner, definitely," Stan replies. "To begin with, you don't want to invest in a board until you're sure you know what kind of board you need. That takes time and trial and error. Also, depending on how fast you advance, the board you buy now might not be right a couple of months from now. Make sure you're riding comfortably before you invest in a board. And make sure the board you buy is right for you."

"Got it," Adam murmurs, writing.

"When you check the edges, be sure you run your fingernail down the board away from the end of your nail. If you run your fingernail the wrong way, you risk getting steel splinters underneath your nails. That can be pretty nasty."

Adam suddenly realizes he's mindlessly rubbing the end of his finger as he visualizes that unfortunate mistake. Stan goes on to explain that a qualified shop will have what's known as a TUNING CENTER, where equipment is tuned. There an equipment professional can file the board's edges each time after they become rough. A snowboarder also should make sure that the bottom surface, or BASE, of the board is smooth and properly waxed.

Stan clarifies: "The base of a board will become nicked as you ride over rocks, ice, and other rough surfaces. You can repair those abrasions by taking a standard hot iron and melting special repair plastic over the abrasive surface. Then use the iron to coat the entire base by melting a special wax over the surface of the base. Smooth out that wax by ironing your board, again just like you would iron a shirt.

"Eventually, when you buy a board, you will learn to file the edges and apply repair plastic and wax yourself. In the beginning, however, rely on a professional to get the job done right. You with me so far?"

"I get it," Adam says. He then asks a question that's been bothering him for the last few minutes. "Is that board warped? Why does it bow in the middle?"

Stan chuckles. "Good observation, but no, it's not warped. All boards are designed with this bow in the middle. It's called the CAMBER, and it's designed to distribute energy and weight. Remember, when you're riding, you're standing on the board, which means the board must absorb all your weight. With the camber, a rider's weight makes the board rest flat on the snow. All the energy is moved throughout the length of the board, sort of like a large shock absorber. Camber is one factor you want to check when getting a board. All other things being equal, a heavy person might want more camber than a lighter person."

"But all other things *aren't* equal, are they?" Adam counters.

Stan smiles, then he explains how snowboards come in four different styles:

- RACE BOARDS,
- CARVING BOARDS,
- FREERIDE BOARDS, and
- FREESTYLE BOARDS.

Adam nods, recognizing that these different boards mirror the different styles of riding he learned from Tara.

Stan explains that race boards are longer and stiffer than the other boards. This gives the race board greater responsiveness at high speeds. Also, race boards have a greater effective edge.

"Hold it," Adam interjects. "What is a greater effective edge? Is it thicker?"

"No," Stan says. "EFFECTIVE EDGE is the amount of edge that's in contact with the snow." Stan retrieves a longer race board and holds it up next to his example board. "Some boards have a slightly upturned nose and tail. This, again, makes them easier to turn and maneuver. Race boards have very little upturn in the nose and virtually no upturn in the tail. That puts more of the board on the snow. These boards require more energy to turn, but because more of the edge is on the snow, race boards move faster and carve more cleanly between race gates."

"So longer boards go faster?" Adam asks.

"Not necessarily," Stan explains. "Longer boards just handle speed better. It's sort of like Formula One

cars and Volkswagens. Even if you were to put a Formula One engine in a Volkswagen, the length of the
Formula One car, the tightness of its suspension, and
its responsiveness will make it handle better than the
modified Volkswagen. Same with race boards. Because they are stiffer and longer with more effective
edge, race boards simply handle speed better than
shorter, more flexible boards. Race boards also have
less sidecut." Stan holds the two boards together so
that Adam can see the difference in sidecuts. "Less
sidecut makes a race board more difficult to turn, but
the turns are cleaner and the board holds better at
high speeds."

Stan goes on to explain that carving boards are
similar to race boards, only more forgiving. Carving
boards are designed to handle speed and carve clean,
precise turns. They aren't as stiff as race boards, and
there is more upturn in the noses and tails of carving
boards, giving them slightly less effective edge.
They're easier to turn but less responsive than race
boards at high speeds. Carving boards are also a little
wider than race boards. Race boards average nineteen
centimeters in width; carving boards are twenty-two
and a half centimeters wide on average. The differences in width, however, can be felt only by extremely proficient riders.

"Is it safe to assume that freeride and freestyle
boards are designed for freeride and freestyle riding?"

"Exactly," Stan affirms. "Freeride boards are a lot
more flexible than carving boards."

"Hold it," Adam says. "It's great to know about

this board flex, but how can I tell if a board is flexible or stiff?"

Stan pulls another board out of the display rack. Sitting the tail on the floor, Stan grabs the nose of the board with his left hand and puts his right hand squarely in the middle of the board. Pushing the center, Stan forces the board to bend and rebound. "By testing boards this way you can compare different flexes," Stan demonstrates. "Now, you can't just pick up a board, flex it, and know whether it's stiff or flexible. It takes a seasoned rider to know board flex that precisely. However, you can compare different boards by bending them with your hands. Even a novice can feel the difference between a stiff racing board and a flexible freeride board."

"And, freeride boards are more flexible so they can turn quicker, right?"

"Sort of. Freeride boards come around quicker and handle shock—like landing a table top—better than the longer, stiffer carving boards. They have a shorter effective edge because the nose and tail are elevated. Comparing freeride boards to carving boards is sort of like comparing the Formula One car to a dune buggy. They serve different purposes. You can race on a freeride board, but you probably won't win. And you can do jumps and ride fakie on some carving boards, but they aren't the best boards for that kind of riding."

Adam takes notes and then inquires, "What is landing a table top?"

Stan nods and spells it out. "TABLE TOPS are flat

areas. Sometimes you will hear riders say they FLAT-BOTTOMED, or bottomed-out, on the table tops. These are jumps that were brought to snowboarding from motocross. Riders catch air off a carved takeoff, then they either jump over or land on a flat area known as a table top before descending into the landing. When you flatbottom on the table top, you don't jump completely over the flat area. It can be jarring. Usually, when you jump, you land on a descending slope, which means the shock of landing is absorbed by the fleeting landscape. It's a real shock when you land flat."

Adam makes a note to avoid table tops for a while. "So, freeride boards are designed for less speed but more maneuverability. Is that right?"

"Yes. Freeride boards are do-it-all boards. In fact, I recommend that you learn on a freeride board because you can progress to a carving board or move to a freestyle board or simply get a longer freeride board once you're riding. Unless you're racing or doing some really radical stuff, freeride boards are always your best bet."

"What about freestyle boards?" Adam asks.

Stan retreats once more to the display rack and retrieves another board, this one shorter and wider than the freeride board. He demonstrates that most freestyle boards have no distinction between the nose and the tail. While the graphics may be directional, the boards themselves are completely symmetrical. That means the boards have less effective edge than the freeride boards and much less than the carving and racing boards.

"These boards are definitely not for racing," Stan says. "In fact, the other major difference between these boards and others is the construction. Manufacturers want to make freestyle boards as light as possible without destroying the weight-to-stiffness ratios, so you'll find all kinds of strange materials in these boards. By using different composite materials, board makers have successfully made boards lighter without sacrificing too much stiffness. Some manufacturers even put aluminum honeycomb with air injections into the nose and tail of their freestyle boards. It's really high tech."

"So, these boards are stiff but light," Adam says.

"Not as stiff as a racing board," Stan says, "but stiffer than they otherwise would be, given their size and weight. Freestyle boards are the most flexible boards, but given what you're trying to accomplish, that's not all bad. Also, the flex patterns on freestyle boards are a little different. With freeride, carving, and race boards, the nose is often a little stiffer than the tail. That makes the board ride forward really well.

"A freestyle board is equally stiff in both the nose and tail, which makes it kind of like a trick water ski: Direction doesn't matter. On a freestyle board you might catch air forward and land backward, or take off backward and land forward, or twist, or whatever. A lot of those spectacular tricks you see on television are performed on freestyle boards."

Adam writes this down and underlines *freeride* as the board he will be riding for a while. Then another question comes to him. "Obviously, I am not looking

THE SNOWBOARD

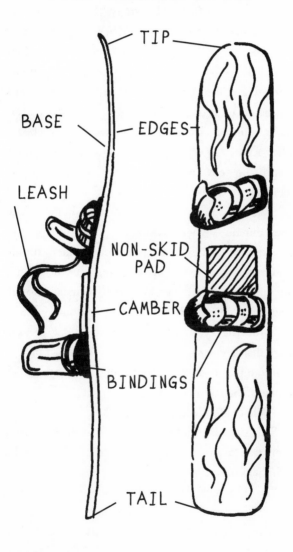

TIP

BASE

EDGES

LEASH

NON-SKID PAD

CAMBER

BINDINGS

TAIL

to become an expert in snowboard construction, but if, as you suggest, I choose to rent a board, what else do I need to look for?"

"Ask how old the board is," Stan replies. "If you're about to rent a board that's more than four years old, ask for a younger one. Board technology has advanced at such a rapid pace that any board older than four years is going to feel like a plank compared to today's boards. Also, some boards are made from recycled old snowboards and skis. They're called RECYCLERS. If you choose one of those, you're supporting recycled products. Other than that, it's personal preference."

Stan goes on to emphasize that it's important to take your time when looking at boards. The prevailing wisdom suggests that prospective riders should spend at least an hour concentrating on what boards are out there. That way, you give yourself enough time to get comfortable with all the options.

"Hopefully, you will be spending all day or even more than a day on your board, so it's a good idea to spend ample up-front time making the right choice of board," Stan concludes.

"What about length?" Adam asks.

Stan steps in front of Adam and makes a cursory estimation of his student's height. "I'd say you need a 155," Stan observes.

"A 155 what?" Adam wants to know.

"A board that's 155 centimeters long. Boards are measured in centimeters, no matter what style you're riding. For example, a 155 freeride is a

BOARDS COME IN DIFFERENT
LENGTHS FOR DIFFERENT
RIDING STYLES AND RIDERS.

GETTING CRAZY
OFF THE BEATEN PATH

PURE SPEED

155-centimeter-long freeride board. Remember, longer boards are usually reserved for carving and racing, and shorter boards are used for tricks and other maneuvers."

"So is 155 the standard length for spastics?" Adam asks with a slight chuckle.

"No," Stan answers. "A beginner of average height and weight should get a board that comes up to his or her chin. I guess you're about 180 centimeters tall, and a 155-centimeter board should come to your chin. A heavier rider probably needs a slightly longer board, and a lighter rider might want a shorter board. Of course, none of this is cast in stone. If you find that you're carving turns quickly and want to move up to a longer, faster board, or you're in deep snow and you find that you need a longer board for cleaner flotation and turning, by all means move up. There is no standard beginner length, just like there is no standard professional length. Professional freestyle riders usually stick with 150s or 155s, while giant slalom racers might use 170s or 175s. Again, a good rule of thumb is to stick to a board that's about chin height, using that as a starting point from which you can then adjust as you gravitate toward a particular discipline."

Adam feverishly writes this down, then looks up to see that Stan has moved away from the display and is walking toward the rear of the store. "Are we done?" he inquires.

"Oh, not by a long shot," Stan retorts. "Assuming you have a board picked out, you still have to stand on it. That requires a lot more work than you probably know."

Adam smiles and follows Stan to the rear of the store where he is fully prepared to learn how to stand and walk all over again.

FOUR

OFF ON THE RIGHT FOOT

Adam looks around the rear of the shop and sees that what he had previously assumed were elaborate hiking boots are, in fact, something quite different. He turns to Stan and remarks, "I take it you wear special boots when you're riding."

"Absolutely," Stan says. "Picking the right board is important, but nothing is more crucial than getting the right boots and bindings."

"Bindings?" Adam repeats.

"Sure. You become one with the board through the bindings, and your board responds to your movements through the boot-binding connection. If you pick a lousy board, you can still ride with some degree of success and fun. If you pick lousy boots and bindings, you're in for a miserable and, maybe, dangerous day."

Stan describes two basic kinds of boot systems and several combinations of bindings for each. The first type of boot he talks about is the HARD BOOT, which, as the name implies, is made of hard, rigid plastic. The boot actually has an outer portion called the SHELL and an inner portion called the LINER. The shell is hard and restrictive and inhibits ankle movement, while the liner is soft and provides cushioning for the rider's foot.

"They look like something out of the Apollo space program," Adam muses, realizing only after he has said it that Stan is probably too young to remember the Apollo moon walks.

Stan nods and continues. "A lot of skiers who cross over to snowboarding choose hard boot setups because ski boots are hard. Also, most racers and carvers wear hard boots because of the greater feel and stability. In fact, some world-champion racers wear ski boots because snowboard boots aren't stiff enough for them. That's not recommended for average riders, though, because ski boots don't provide enough lateral ankle movement. Most people can't turn a board at all wearing ski boots."

"So, the hard-boot system gives you more stability, but it's harder to turn," Adam adds.

"Exactly," Stan says. "Hard boots are more responsive, but the motion required to make a turn is much different than in soft boots. It's tougher to get the board around, and as a result you won't find many freestyle riders riding in hard boots. Riders in hard boots must adjust buckles so that the boot does not slip or rub."

Adam looks bewildered. Stan realizes he needs to backtrack a little. "Hard boots have to close tightly around your shin to support your ankle and foot. It isn't like a shoe, where you simply untie the laces and slip your foot in under the tongue. The shell of a hard boot opens on a hinge so that your foot can slip inside. That shell is then locked by a series of buckles that hold it in place. When fitting hard boots, make sure that the buckles are latched so that your foot is secure, yet you still have enough freedom of movement to get around.

"No matter what kind of boot you're in, you want to make sure it fits snugly. As a rule, people get boots too big. That usually causes problems out on the mountain."

"So, get a snug-fitting boot," Adam says.

"Get a boot that fits without a lot of free room inside. When you're trying on boots in the shop, get a pair that initially feels uncomfortably small. Walk around in them for at least a half hour. Whether you're in hard boots or soft boots, you want to spend a lot of time in the boots to make absolutely sure they fit properly. This isn't just for comfort, it's for safety. You rely on your boot as your connector. It's what enables you to initiate turns and ride in control. Without proper fitting, you're lost before you ever get started."

Adam writes this down. "Okay, I think I understand hard boots. How do you attach the boots to the board?"

Stan picks up a board that has what Adam assumes are bindings attached to its top side. The attachments resemble small dumbbell bars with clips on each end. "Hard boots require what's known as PLATE BINDINGS," Stan explains. "Plate bindings clip the boot in place at the toe and the heel."

Stan picks up a hard boot and demonstrates the procedure for locking it into the binding. The heel goes in first, clipping into the back of the barbell-shaped structure. Then the toe is pressed down and the front of the binding flips up to lock the boot into place.

Adam smiles and reflects, "It doesn't look like that's going anywhere."

"Hopefully, it won't," Stan says. "Obviously, plate bindings have to be adjusted to fit individual boots. That's something you want to make sure is done properly before you go out on the mountain. Again, boots and bindings are what connect you to the board. You don't want to lose that connection."

Adam looks once more at the plate binding. "So, does this binding release when you fall?"

"No," Stan asserts. "That's one of the big differences between snowboarding and skiing. Almost none of the binding systems in snowboarding release when you fall. You stay with your board at all times. The good news is that this connection, along with the fact that both feet are attached to the same board, cuts down on rotary joint injuries—sprained ankles and knees—that are common in skiing."

Adam nods his head. He might be a thrill-seeker, but he's not stupid. "Okay, that takes care of hard boot and plate bindings. I assume the other kind of system is—"

"Soft boot," Stan interrupts. "The soft-boot system is much more common among beginners and nonracers, in part because it's more forgiving than the rigid hard-boot system. Also, it's easier to make freestyle maneuvers in soft boots. You have a lot more flexibility in the ankles."

Stan retrieves a soft boot. Adam immediately notices that it resembles a hiking or standard-issue combat boot. There are laces in the front, and the sides appear to be much more flexible. There are no hard plastic shell and buckles or braces that have to be latched.

"That does look more comfortable," Adam observes.

"More comfortable but designed for a different function," Stan continues. "Soft-boot systems don't give you the precise responsiveness and sensitive feel that you get with a hard-boot system, but it is much easier to make quick moves and turns in soft boots. Freeride and freestyle riders use soft-boot systems.

"To use the car analogy again, the hard-boot, plate-binding system is like a race car on a smooth asphalt track. You wouldn't drive that car in the Baja 500. Likewise, you wouldn't put a dune buggy on a track with race cars. The soft-boot system is like a dune buggy. You cut, jump, jib, and catch air in soft boots, and you carve long, smooth, fast turns in hard boots."

"What if you don't plan on doing either? I expect to be on my tush for a while, so which system is best for me?"

"It's a matter of personal preference. Unless you have some strong personal reasons for learning in hard boots, the comfort and versatility of soft boots make them preferable. You also will find that once you start linking turns you won't have as much CHATTER in soft boots as you might experience in hard boots."

"Chatter?"

"Yeah. Chatter is like turbulence on an airplane: It's the vibration and skidding you get when carving a turn at high speed. It's not something to worry about yet, but it is something you might want to file away in your head."

Adam duly writes his recommendation down in the notepad. "What about soft-boot bindings?" he asks. "I assume there are different bindings for soft boots as well."

"You assume right," Stan says, further explaining that unlike hard-boot setups, riders have several options when it comes to soft-boot bindings:

- There is the standard SHELL BINDING, which resembles a hard plastic sandal attached to the board. This binding has a moderately high plastic back against which riders place the heels of their boots. Straps hold the toe of the boot in place, and the hard plastic back supports the ankle and lower leg.

- Another form of shell binding is called the HIGH-BACK system. This binding looks just like the standard shell binding, except that the hard plastic back is higher.

BOOTS AND BINDINGS

HARD   SOFT

RACERS LIKE HARD BOOTS,
BUT STYLING RIDERS PREFER
SOFT BOOTS.

DISK   HIGH-BACK

- Now manufacturers are coming out with SKY BACK-systems, which are shell systems but with the plastic back extending up to the rider's calf muscle. These systems restrict ankle movement, which is why they are not preferred by extreme freestyle riders, but they do provide more support.

- Recently, manufacturers have created STEP-IN bindings for soft boots. In these step-in systems, the hard plastic backing is built into the boot. A ring on the inside portion of the boot is slipped through a hook and a locking clip fastens the outside of the boot to the binding. These bindings are easy and convenient. Because the hard plastic backing is built into the boot, they are more comfortable than shell bindings.

"So, you recommend I go with a step-in system?" Adam inquires.

"Spend a lot of time in your boots checking out the different systems before you make any decisions," Stan suggests. "Each system has its own advantages and disadvantages. Don't assume what's right for one person is right for everyone. Take your time and make your own decisions."

"Okay," Adam says. "Is that all there is to bindings?"

"Not hardly," Stan acknowledges. "Assuming you've picked your boot and binding system, now you have to mount the bindings to fit your stance."

"My stance?"

"Yes." Stan puts a bindless board down on the

floor. "Stand on that board and imagine you're riding down a hill."

Adam does as instructed, assuming his normal athletic stance and posture—knees slightly bent, feet apart, weight evenly distributed, head up, eyes ahead, and hands in front of him.

"Good," Stan says. "You're a little stinky, but that's okay."

"Stinky?!" Adam reacts. "How can stinky be okay?"

Stan laughs and explains that stinky means Adam's stance is a little wide. That style of riding is called STINKBUG, or STINKY. A stinkbug is a large insect that walks with its back legs disproportionately far apart. When a rider takes a wider-than-shoulder-width stance, it's called a stinkbug stance, and that rider is referred to as stinky. Some of the best riders in the world are stinky.

Adam shakes his head and laughs. "It's hard to imagine stinky being good, but I get it."

"Good," Stan says. "More important than being a stinkbug, however, is the angle of your feet on the board."

Adam looks down at his feet. "What about it?"

"We want to set your feet so that you can learn to turn and maneuver, but we don't want to set your stance too strong or too weak." Adam gives another confused look and Stan hesitates before clarifying. "Imagine you are standing on the face of a round protractor, like the face of a clock, only instead of minutes or seconds the face is divided into degrees."

BINDINGS CONNECT THE BOARD TO THE RIDER.

"Okay," Adam mumbles, conjuring up long-lost images from high-school geometry.

Stan spells it out. "If you place both your feet straight across the board so that your toes point straight over the side, you are standing at zero degrees. If you are standing with both feet pointed toward the nose of the board, you are standing at ninety degrees. Nobody in snowboarding rides at ninety degrees, and very few people ride at zero degrees. A lot of people ride between fifteen and fifty degrees, however, and it's important to know how you want to ride."

As Adam listens to Stan, he begins to get a good feel for how foot-placement angles relate to snowboarding performance. Before going out on the mountain, a snowboarder should mount the bindings according to whatever stance he or she wants to take. Such a stance is measured in degrees, front foot first, back foot second. A stance of fifty-five, forty-five, for example, has the front foot positioned at fifty-five degrees and the back foot positioned at forty-five degrees. That's a preferred carving stance. Race-board and carving stances generally run between forty-five and sixty degrees, putting the rider in a faster position. A good freeriding stance has the front foot between thirty and thirty-five degrees, and the back foot between fifteen and thirty degrees.

"Sometimes you'll find people who set their back foot at zero degrees, and set their front foot at fifteen or twenty degrees," Stan elaborates, "and sometimes you'll find people who ride what's known as DUCK.

That's where the back foot is actually turned out less than zero degrees. It's very tough to turn from those neutral or duck positions, but they are also very stable stances for doing tricks. Most freestyle professionals—those you see performing amazing jumps, grabs, twists, and flips—ride a front-foot angle of between twenty and thirty degrees, and a back-foot angle of between five and ten degrees."

"I've never been out at all. How do I know what stance I need?" Adam follows up.

"A good, middle-of-the-road freeride stance for novices is forty, twenty-five—that's forty degrees on the front foot and twenty-five degrees on the back foot. If you find you're more comfortable with a stronger or weaker stance once you're on the mountain, take your board into the local shop and have your bindings adjusted. Four quick turns with a screwdriver and the binding angles can be reset. Experiment as much as necessary in order to get comfortable."

Adam draws the face of a sundial in his notepad and labels the degrees, marking his middle-of-the road stance for future reference. He is about to ask another question when Stan says something that catches him off-guard.

"I want you to run across the floor and pretend you're trying to stop quickly on a sheet of ice."

Adam dutifully runs across the shop floor and abruptly stops while trying to imagine a sheet of ice beneath his feet. His stance is wide and awkward— "stinky," as Stan would say—but that's not what Stan is examining.

"You're goofy, but that's okay, too," Stan laughs.

"Hold it," Adam says. "First I'm stinky, now I'm goofy, and both of these are okay? I'll need group therapy before getting out of here."

Both laugh, and Stan says, "GOOFY means you are right-foot-forward. What you just did, running across the floor and pretending to stop on ice, is called the GOOFY TEST. Had I told you why you were doing it, you would have thought about it and the test wouldn't have been accurate. Your brain works a certain way when it comes to which foot should be forward when riding. Even though most people are right-handed, 70 percent of all people who take the goofy test are REGULAR; that is, they lead with their left foot. You, me, and 30 percent of the population are goofy-footed: We lead with our right foot."

"Is one any better than the other?" Adam asks, assuming that anything called "goofy" has to be a handicap.

"Not at all," Stan assures him. "It's just the way your brain works."

Adam looks at all his notes and attempts to sum up where he is at this point. "So, I'm a stinky, goofy-footed, soft-boot freerider who stands at forty, twenty-five on a 155 recycler."

"That you are, my friend," Stan affirms, patting Adam on the back as he defines some other relevant terms for Adam:

- TOE EDGE and TOE TURN, which are, as the names imply, the edge of the board near your toes and a turn toward that edge;

THE STANCE

A RIGHT-FOOT-FORWARD STANCE IS CALLED A GOOFY AND A LEFT-FOOT-FORWARD STANCE IS CALLED REGULAR OR STRAIGHT.
A WIDER-THAN-SHOULDER-WIDTH STANCE IS CALLED STINK BUG.

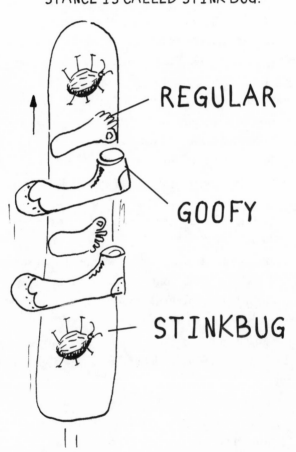

- HEEL EDGE and HEEL TURN, which are the edge of the board near your heels and turning toward that edge;
- FRONTSIDE, which is the side you're facing; and
- BACKSIDE, which is the side you're not facing.

Adam then asks, "Why wouldn't you just say toe side or heel side, instead of frontside and backside?"

"It primarily has to do with tricks," Stan explains. "Toe and heel refer to turns and the edges of your board, while frontside and backside refer to sides where tricks, slides, and other things might happen. It's a subtle distinction, but one that will show others that you know your stuff.

"Okay," Stan announces, clapping his hands to indicate a change in the subject. "Let's get you suited up in the right attire so that you can put all of this knowledge to good use."

Stan walks Adam back to the front of the shop where a tall young woman is completing a sale and wishing another customer a good day. "Hey, Michelle, have you got a minute?" Stan calls.

The young woman walks over and introduces herself as Michelle Tigger. After a few opening pleasantries, she says to Adam, "Tara was telling me you're riding for the first time in a couple of weeks."

"That's right," Adam acknowledges. "I'm trying to learn enough so I don't make a fool of myself out there."

"Which is where you come in, Michelle," Stan adds. "I was hoping you could help us out by showing Adam apparel and accessories." He turns back to

Adam. "I assume since you don't ski, you don't own any ski clothes."

"You got that right," Adam admits. "I wouldn't know where to start."

"Follow me," Michelle declares, and she and Adam retreat to another area of the Wild Ride Snowboard Shop.

FIVE

CARVING-EDGE FASHION

"I guess you want to be fashionable as well as functional out there," Michelle says, leading Adam into an area of the shop littered with clothing displays, hanging racks, and accessory cases.

"I haven't really considered it," Adam replies. "I don't know how fashionable you can be when you're on your back in the snow. It would be kind of silly of me to dress like a champion and ride like a dunce."

Michelle laughs at this, then turns serious. "It doesn't cost any more to be fashionable. The important thing is to be prepared. Fashion is one thing, FROSTBITE is another. Riding can be the experience of your life, but don't ever forget that a snow-covered mountain is the most hostile environment on the planet, more dangerous than the desert, the ocean, or the jungle. If you're prepared, you can have a great time. If you're not, you can injure yourself quickly and permanently."

This is serious business, and Michelle now has Adam's undivided attention. "What do I need?" he appeals. "I have a heavy coat, but I don't think I have anything you would consider winter-sport appropriate."

"You want to start by considering the elements and what you will be doing," she cautions. "Dress for warmth, but also keep in mind that riding is physical. You have to be able to move, and you're going to work up a sweat. You want to think about how to dress in order to balance all those factors.

"The first step in that process is to dress in layers. You might have the greatest winter coat in the world that keeps you so warm you need only a T-shirt underneath it. Unfortunately, if you wear something like that on the mountain, you're dead meat."

"Why's that?"

"Because halfway through your first run you're going to be wringing wet with sweat—and the T-shirt will be soaked. Because the coat keeps the moisture next to you, your body will chill. You will want to take the coat off; but if you do that, you'll freeze. In short, you'll be a miserable wreck before you get down the hill your first time."

"Okay, so assuming what I currently own is useless, how do I dress for success out there?"

Michelle suggests to Adam that he start thinking in terms of three distinct layers of clothing, each with a different function:

- First, wear a layer next to your skin that wicks moisture and moves it away from your body. This wicking layer can be polypropylene

underwear or any of a number of specially designed synthetics. Cotton is not good because,
while it absorbs, it *holds* moisture rather than
moving it away.

- Your second layer should absorb the moisture
that the first layer just moved away from your
skin. This is where fleece and wool come in
handy. A sweater or another shirt with more
absorption qualities will add a much-needed
layer of insulation.

- The third layer has several functions: (1) It insu-
lates, keeping warmth in; (2) it breathes, letting
perspiration evaporate; and (3) it should keep
outside moisture from getting next to your
skin. Remember, snow is wet. If you allow wet,
cold snow to penetrate your clothing, you've
defeated the whole purpose. A material like
Gortex, which is porous enough to let air particles pass through but fine enough to repel water
particles, is perfect but expensive. There are
other synthetics out there that achieve the same
results at a reasonable price, but the objective is
to stay warm and dry while still being able to
move. Always think in layers.

"Three layers is a good rule of thumb," Michelle
notes, "but it's not always true. You have to use common sense. Some days the temperature is downright
balmy. I've seen people riding in bathing suits. Some
days it's so cold you need four, maybe five layers just
to keep the wind out. The best rule is to always be
prepared and pay attention to your environment."

"Noted," Adam says as he reviews his notes. "You know, Michelle," he adds, "I can come up with some underwear that wicks moisture away, and I own more than my fair share of sweaters and turtlenecks, but I'm not sure I know what I need for that outer layer."

Michelle smiles, motioning him over to a display, where Adam is struck by the designs and patterns he sees in jackets, pants, and outerwear. "Outerwear comes in more styles and designs than you can imagine," Michelle shows him, "but don't sacrifice performance for something that looks good." She points to a mannequin racer charging down an imaginary run. The figurine looks to be wearing a tie-dyed wet suit. Adds Michelle, "If you really get into the sport you can consider buying a race suit like this one. It's the most expensive outerwear you can buy, but when you reach a point where feeling every motion counts, this type of suit is something to consider."

In the meantime, Michelle encourages Adam to start with standard snowboard pants:

- SNOWBOARD PANTS are generally baggy to give you plenty of room for other layers. They are made from water-repellent, breathable materials, and they have extra padding in the seat and knees. That padding is one of the big differences between snowboard pants and ski pants. Don't be alarmed by this revelation: Novices are going to fall a lot, at least in the first few hours. This extra padding helps keep the rider dry and comfortable. Also, well-padded, well-positioned pockets with either zipper or Velcro closures are very important. Don't plan to carry a lot of items in the pockets, but things like camera film, a watch, and maybe a candy bar or other high-energy food items are sensible.

- When shopping for a JACKET, don't get the bulkiest parka available. If you look like a snowman, you'll move like one. Acquire something roomy so more layers can be added underneath. It should also be waterproof and warm. Make sure such a jacket extends below the waist and is sturdy enough to withstand the aggressive, physical movements of riding. Check the stitching, the zippers, the collar, and the cuffs to make sure nothing harmful is exposed, such as a zipper next to the throat or heavy buttons near the wrists. Look for a jacket with a hood, which can be a lifesaver when you're caught in a storm. Finally, one of the features unique to snowboarding jackets is underarm zippers called PIT-ZIPS. These offer the means to air out perspiration.

Adam feverishly writes all this down, then turns to Michelle and inquires, "Is that it?"

"Not by a long shot," she retorts. Michelle explains to Adam that in hostile winter conditions it's imperative to keep your extremities covered. Waterproof gloves or mittens are a must. "Mittens are actually preferable," she says. "It's a little tougher to pick things up or to operate zippers with mittens, but you aren't doing much of that during a run anyway. Mittens keeps all your fingers together so they share body heat. That makes a big difference when the temperature dips down below freezing and you intend to stay outside for an extended period of time."

"Got it," Adam notes.

"Another extremity you want to keep covered is your head, not just for the sake of warmth, but for safety." Michelle reaches over to a nearby shelf and removes one of many multicolored helmets that look remarkably like the helmets Adam wears when sky diving. "You need to wear a helmet," she says. "To keep your head warm you need a knit ski cap, but a helmet can keep you alive if you crash and burn. I don't want to sound like a doomsayer, but part of the thrill of riding is pushing the limits. In those situations a helmet can save your life."

Adam nods. "I wear helmets in other activities, so that's nothing new."

"Good," she affirms, before going into details about other forms of protection Adam needs to be aware of:

- Wear GOGGLES or SUNGLASSES in all circumstances, even if the sun is hidden behind a cloud bank. Snow is like a mirror: You can be riding along thinking you don't need eye protection, and before you know it, you've burned your cornea and are suffering from SNOW BLINDNESS. This can be a major medical problem. Vented, dual-thermopane goggles are the best. Besides providing eye protection, they offer insulation and warmth for your face. Because of the dual panes, they won't fog up like some less-

ACCESSORIES

FLEECE JACKET
(WORN UNDER SHELL)

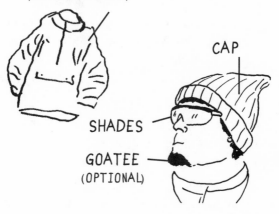

CAP

SHADES

GOATEE
(OPTIONAL)

OUTER JACKET
WITH PIT-ZIPS
(REMOVABLE SLEEVES)

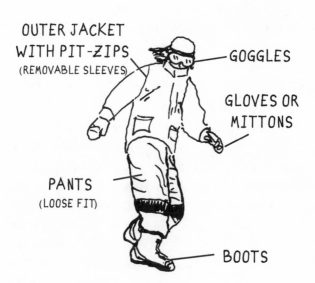

GOGGLES

GLOVES OR
MITTONS

PANTS
(LOOSE FIT)

BOOTS

expensive goggles or glasses. If you simply want to buy sunglasses, pick a pair with treated ultra-violet lenses that also resist fogging. Don't skimp.

- Another important accessory is sunscreen. Snow reflects the sun's rays more directly than both sand and water, regardless of the tempera-ture or cloud conditions. If you don't wear sun-screen, your skin is going to cook and you are going to be miserable.

"Okay," Adam says. "I think I'm covered head to toe now."

"Not quite," she cautions. "Head we've covered; toes we haven't. You still need socks."

"I have a drawer full," Adam counters.

"Plan on adding at least one more pair," she says. "Snowboarding socks are specially designed to keep your feet warm, wick moisture away, and provide feel inside your boot. A lot of people make the mistake of wearing thick wool socks or two pairs of cotton socks. Don't. Your only connection with your board is through your feet, and feel is critical. Trying to ride in two pairs of socks or heavy wool socks is like trying to shoot a basketball while wearing boxing gloves. It doesn't work. One good pair of snowboarding socks will keep you warm and give you the feel you need to turn and move your board."

"Anything else?" he asks while writing.

"You might want to consider knee pads and wrist guards," she recommends. "You're going to take some spills out there, especially if you push the limits. You're going to fall either on your butt or your knees. Your

GOGGLES OR SUNGLASSES
ARE A MUST TO
PREVENT SNOWBLINDNESS.

butt has plenty of padding built in; your knees don't. Any good snowboard shop will carry special knee pads that provide protection but still allow you to move. The same is true with wrist guards. Whether you fall forward or backward, you're going to brace yourself with your hands. Wrist injuries can be common, so wrist guards are something you want to seriously consider."

"Gotcha," he acknowledges. He's pleased by her quick assessment of his personality. He will almost *certainly* push the limits. "Any other accessories?"

Michelle responds by mentioning some nonessentials that can at least make for added convenience:

- lip balm, to protect your lips the same way sunscreen protects the face;
- a WAIST PACK, or FANNY PACK, for long treks or if hiking to a remote area. It's always good to carry water and some additional nourishment if you're going to be out a while. These packs allow you to carry additional supplies without adding too much bulk.
- a good attitude. Nothing improves the snowboarding experience like taking on the challenge with the proper frame of mind. This is a great sport that can, quite literally, lead to a number of lifestyle changes.

Adam ponders all this as he thanks Michelle for everything and returns to the main part of the shop, where Tara and Stan are waiting.

"So, did you find everything you need?" Stan asks.

"I think so," Adam replies. "I can't think of any more questions, so I guess I'm ready to go."

"Oh, no, you're not," Tara says. "How are you going to get to the mountain? Who is going to give you your first lesson? Have you ever bought a lift ticket? Do you even know what a lift ticket is? Have you thought about what you're going to do after your first day? What if your group wants to ride another mountain? Are you going with them?"

Adam is taken aback by all these questions and he looks at both Tara and Stan. "I guess I don't know as much as I thought."

"Good thing you came to see us," Stan says. "While you were off getting a fashion lesson, I set up a meeting for you with one of our best instructors. He'll fill you in on the basics you need to know before getting to the mountain."

Six

Riding Lessons

Stan motions Adam toward an office in the back of the shop. "Adam, I'd like you to meet Jeff Brashy, the best snowboard instructor in the area and a good friend of the Wild Ride Snowboard Shop," Stan declares with great fervor. "Jeff, this is our student Adam, the guy who before today knew absolutely nothing about snowboarding."

Jeff jumps up from a metal folding chair and extends a large, weathered hand. "Nice to meet you, Adam," he says. "I take it you know more than nothing now."

"Slightly," Adam answers. "I know what sort of equipment and accessories I need, but I don't have a clue what to do next."

Jeff smiles and asks for Adam to take a seat in another folding chair near a small, cluttered metal desk. "So, you've decided to enter the snowboard life," Jeff says as he returns to his seat. "We were all beginners once. You'll find snowboarders to be some of the friendliest, most patient people on the mountain, partly because the snowboard lifestyle is just naturally friendly and partly because snowboarders were out- casts for so long. The fraternity of riders is only too eager to welcome new members."

"Outcasts?" Adam asks.

"Oh, yes," Jeff replies. "For years, snowboards were considered dangerous, and riders were looked down on as reckless hotshots who had no business being anywhere near respectable skiers. Most resorts restricted or even banned boards. Fortunately, all that has changed. Now there are very few moun- tains that bar access to riders. In fact, most have de- signed special areas just for riders. Resorts go to great lengths to attract snowboarders. Are you get- ting a group discount?"

"No. I didn't know there were such things," Adam admits.

"Oh, yes. Most mountains offer special lift-ticket packages to groups. Check it out."

"What's a LIFT TICKET?" Adam inquires.

Jeff can't believe his ears. "You really do know absolutely nothing."

"Told ya," Adam says.

"Okay, let's start from the beginning," Jeff con- tinues. "Once you've rented your equipment and bought your clothes, what do you plan to do next?"

"Go ride at the local resort," Adam answers.

"How are you going to get your board there?"

Adam gives Jeff a puzzled look. "In the trunk of my car, I guess," he says, not sure where this is leading.

"You're probably right," Jeff agrees. "One of the great advantages to snowboarding and one of the reasons it has grown so much faster than skiing is its convenience. With snowboarding you just have your board, your boots, and yourself. Even so, you still want to make sure you have enough room to properly transport your board."

Adam nods and observes, "I've chosen a 155 freestyle, so it should fit in the back of my hatchback."

"Probably, but make sure," Jeff says. "Also, you want to schedule your first lesson before you arrive at the mountain." Jeff explains two options when it comes to lessons:

- A GROUP LESSON is, as the name implies, a lesson with a group of people. You can sign up for group lessons at the mountain. The upside to group lessons is being with kindred spirits who want to learn. The downside is that the lesson can only progress as fast as the slowest person in the group, and no one receives a great deal of individual attention from the instructor. Group lessons are generally less expensive, but sometimes they can be less effective as well.

- PRIVATE LESSONS are more expensive, but the instruction is more personalized. You can progress at your own rate. Instructors usually charge hourly rates or, in some instances, half-day or full-day rates. Make sure, however, you feel comfortable with the instructor before committing to half-day or full-day tutorials.

LESSONS

INDIVIDUAL LESSONS ARE MORE EXPEN-
SIVE, BUT YOU PROGRESS
AT YOUR OWN PACE.
GROUP LESSONS ARE LESS EXPENSIVE,
BUT YOU GET LESS PERSONAL
ATTENTION.

INDIVIDUAL
LESSONS

GROUP
LESSONS

"If I know nothing, how can I be qualified to judge an instructor?" Adam asks.

Jeff tells Adam to ask questions. Ask the instructor how many beginners he or she has taught. How long has the instructor been teaching? Another important question is, how long has the instructor been employed at a particular resort? Of course, there are dozens of other sensible questions, too.

"Certainly, you would ask pointed questions when a surgeon is about to operate on you," Jeff opines.

"Good point," Adam says. "But doctors have credentials, certifications, and things like M.D. after their names."

"The same is true with snowboard instructors," Jeff notes. "Insist on an instructor who has been certified by the Professional Snowboard Instructors Association—the PSIA. When you see those words or that acronym, you know the teacher has gone through extensive training and passed a series of tests. Too often people rely on friends or people they know who are proficient riders, but not true instructors. That's a mistake. Hire someone who not only is proficient and certified, but who specializes in beginners."

Adam then asks what he should expect from his first lesson.

"Plan on spending a fair amount of time on your butt," Jeff chuckles. "Snowboarding has a shorter, steeper learning curve than skiing. If you're a beginning skier, you can take a lesson, practice for a couple of hours, and be skiing at a decent beginning level by the end of your first day. You won't be good, but you will be able to move down the slopes without falling too often.

"Snowboarding is different. You spend a lot of time falling, picking yourself up, and falling again. There is a much shorter yet steeper learning curve in snowboarding than there is in skiing. If you're a beginning skier, you can take a lesson, practice for a couple of hours, and be skiing at a decent beginning level by the end of the first day. You won't really be that good, but you will be able to work your way down the slopes.

"It takes a little longer on the front end to learn snowboarding, and that can be frustrating. But that frustration will be short-lived: The good news is that once you start linking turns, you will progress much faster than beginning skiers do because you will have then crossed the one major hurdle to snowboarding proficiency. Most snowboarders go straight from novice to intermediate, completely skipping the lengthy beginner stage that skiers go through."

"So, it takes longer to get started, but you learn quicker once you get the hang of it," Adam states.

"Exactly," Jeff concurs. "Once you get the feel for edging and turning your board, you'll be shredding the mountain with people who have been riding for years."

Adam nods. He's not opposed to a little humility mixed with hard work in learning a new sport. He just wants to learn as much as he can before he straps on a board at the mountain. Which brings up another point.

RIDING HAS A STEEPER LEARNING
CURVE. IT TAKES LONGER TO GET
STARTED, BUT ONCE YOU'RE
RIDING YOU PROGRESS QUICKLY.
DON'T GET FRUSTRATED!

"Okay, what about those lift tickets? How do those work?" Adam asks.

Jeff explains that lift tickets are just like movie tickets or theme park tickets: They give you access to that particular attraction, in this case the mountain. You pay for them at a centralized ticket window. Because daily lift tickets are usually adhesive, like mailing labels, they can be stuck to a WICKET, a hook that attaches to the jacket or pants for easy visibility. Most mountains also sell weekly and seasonal passes. Those are usually laminated plastic badges. Some even have your picture on them to keep them safe from loss or theft. These badges are either mounted to your clothing or worn around your neck so that lift attendants can confirm you have paid your way.

Some lift tickets are included in the price of the first lesson. Call ahead to inquire about the mountain's lift-ticket policies and costs. Like airlines and hotels, most resorts have different rates for different seasons or discounts for different times of day. Some even offer advanced-purchase and group-purchase rates. Be a smart shopper and you can find great rates at most resorts around the world.

"I don't think I'll be traveling anywhere for a while," Adam remarks.

"Don't be so sure," Jeff counters. "Snowboarding is like a drug: Once you get hooked, you'll be seeking out new mountains and new runs. Before long you'll be traveling to some pretty awesome destinations."

"Such as?" Adam says.

IF OUTDOOR LIFE IS YOUR THING, YOU CAN RIDE ALL OVER THE WORLD!

Jeff waves his arms in a large sweeping motion. "You can ride all over the world. There isn't a single part of the world that doesn't have at least one mountain to ride. A lot of professionals travel throughout North America from Christmas through early spring, then immediately go to New Zealand or the Andes where it's fall. Serious riders stay south of the equator until September or October and then go to Europe for some first-snow runs in the Alps. Throw in a few trips to the Himalayas and one or two ventures to Alaska and you've got yourself a pretty full, fun year of intense riding."

Adam looks up from his notes. "Sounds intensely expensive," he says.

"It can be, but it doesn't have to be," Jeff counters. "Snowboarding is an outdoor life. Lots of riders, even professionals, incorporate camping, cooking out-doors, and other cost-saving activities into their trips. It not only cuts costs, it also reinforces the natural as-pects of the sport. I've known guys who don't even have an address: They travel from campsite to camp-site and ride wherever there's snow."

Now, Adam thinks, *you're talking my language.* His free-spirit side is getting motivated the more Jeff talks. Adam used to own a Harley-Davidson motor-cycle, and he always thought it would be great to put a sleeping bag on the back of the bike and spend a year seeing the country. This snowboarding thing might just be the release his wandering spirit needs. He thanks Jeff and stands, assuming he's finished for the day.

"Just one more thing," Adam says. "I understand that a lift ticket gets me on the lift, but I'm not really sure I know what a lift is. Is that what gets you to the top of the mountain?"

Jeff cocks his head and briefly ponders the naiveté of his student. "Have a seat," Jeff says while motioning toward the metal chair. "We've still got a few things to discuss."

SEVEN

A RIDE IN THE PARK

Jeff rummages around on the cluttered desk until he finds what appears to be a folded road map. He unfolds it and Adam sees that it's a detailed schematic of a mountain, with various areas shaded in green, blue, or black.

"This is called a trail map," Jeff points out. "Before you set foot on the snow, you need to pick up one of these maps and have a good look."

"What am I seeing here?"

"This is a complete illustration of a resort," Jeff answers. "It shows all the trails, lifts, and lodges, and it also indicates the difficulty of each run."

Using a pencil, Jeff points out to Adam the BASE LODGE, the building at the base of the mountain that houses instructors' offices, a restaurant, lockers and locker rooms, and a shop filled with equipment and apparel. Near the top of the mountain, Jeff points out, is another lodge, which also has rest rooms and a restaurant. Many riders like taking short breaks in the upper lodge before embarking on lengthy runs. The views from up there can be incredible.

Jeff goes on to explain how to read the trail map and decipher its markings of trail difficulty:

- GREEN CIRCLES, or green markings, are usually reserved for easier, more open, beginner slopes.
- BLUE SQUARES, or blue markings, are for intermediate slopes. These slopes are a little steeper, a little longer, and offer more of a challenge than the beginning slopes.
- Slopes marked with BLACK DIAMONDS are for advanced riders.
- DOUBLE BLACK DIAMONDS are for experts.

Adam studies the trail map, then asks, "Do I need a compass so I can reference my location on this map?"

Jeff laughs. "No, but you have to pay attention to the signs and markings on the mountain. Once you've studied the trail map and figured out which run you want to take, follow the signs posted throughout the mountain. Beware: A lot of trails intersect. If you don't pay attention, you could end up on some sick double-black-diamond runs when you meant to stay on green beginner slopes."

Adam sits up and takes note. "Are these colors universal, or if I go to another resort am I going to see purple or hot-pink runs?"

"Most resorts conform to the green, blue, and black color scheme," Jeff assures Adam, "but in Europe, black-diamond runs are sometimes marked in red. You might find an exception out there, so it's important to get a trail map and study the color key."

Adam asks Jeff about other markings, and Jeff goes into more detail:

- Trails intersect. When approaching an intersection of two or more slopes, you will likely see a sign with a black *X* on a yellow triangle. This means other riders and skiers are merging or crossing your path.

- Be aware of warning posts. These are black-and-yellow-striped poles, usually crossed in the snow to form an *X*. These poles signify the presence of rocks, stumps, crevices, or other dangerous obstacles. Dangerous areas are often roped off. Never cross into roped areas.

- Be on the lookout for black-and-yellow-checkered or plain black flags. These indicate potential avalanche areas. Riders, even expert riders, are killed in avalanches every year.

Adam looks up and tries to hide his alarm. "So, what exactly happens in an avalanche?"

Jeff explains that large sections of snow are often held onto mountainsides by compaction and other forces that seemingly defy gravity. An avalanche results when a large section of snow is dislodged from the side of a mountain. The snow tumbles down the mountain, gaining momentum and knocking down anything in its path, including skiers, snowboarders, mountain climbers, and any other unlucky soul who happens to be in the way.

"Sometimes you will hear riders refer to SLUFF, or being sluffed out," Jeff says. "Sluff is a miniavalanche created by the rider. When carving a turn, you

THE MOUNTAIN

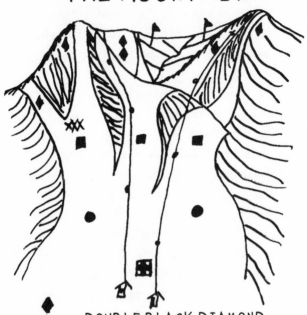

♦
♦   **DOUBLE BLACK DIAMOND**
-VERY DIFFICULT

♦   **BLACK DIAMOND**
-DIFFICULT

■   **INTERMEDIATE BLUE**
-CHALLENGING

●   **BEGINNER GREEN**
-EASY

⊞   **FIRST AID**

XXX   **CROSSING POLES**
-DANGEROUS AREA

⊦   **AVALANCHE DANGER**
-AVALANCHE AREA

displace a certain amount of snow. On a very steep run, that displaced snow slides down the mountain. After two or three turns the amount of displaced snow increases to where it's a small avalanche. If the rider isn't careful, he or she will turn into the sluff and be overtaken by it. That's called being sluffed out. It's not something a beginner needs to fret over, but it's good to know for the future."

"I guess there aren't many avalanches on the beginner slopes," Adam comments.

"Almost never, but always be aware of the dangers. Riding is fun, but it can be deadly if you don't pay attention.

"Of course, the ultimate goal for any beginning rider is to end up in the TERRAIN PARK."

"What's that?" Adam asks.

Jeff elaborates: "A lot of resorts realized that snowboard riders were a different breed with different requirements than skiers. Riders are attracted to jumps, banks, and other physical obstacles that make the average skier wince. Resort owners realized this, so they built special slopes—terrain parks—specifically for freeriding and freestyling. These areas usually have a half pipe, as well as jumps and banks."

Adam's blank expression tells Jeff that he's getting ahead of his pupil, so he slows down to explain more of these strange terms:

- A HALF PIPE is an area of snow carved out to resemble the bottom of a large pipe. The walls of the half pipe slope up until they are vertical. The result is what appears to be the lower half of a large culvert pipe covered with snow. Actually, there is no pipe at all—just packed, sculpted snow.

- JUMPS and TABLE TOPS are ramps and plateaus interspersed throughout the park, where riders can jump and land on a downsloping ramp, also made of snow.

- OBSTACLES are man-made structures on the park. Riders occasionally want to perform tricks off objects such as picnic tables, old cars, and hand rails. This is called JIBBING. Most people believe that jibbing is a carryover from skateboarding, where tables, cars, stairs, and handrails are common obstacles. Also, words like BONK, which means to hit the nose or tail of your board on something, and OLLIE, which means to catch air without actually going off a jump, are carryovers from that same skateboard mind-set.

"Whether you're jibbing, jumping, or trying a 360 tail grab in the half pipe, the terrain park is the ultimate place to be," Jeff points out.

"Noted," Adam says, writing.

"No matter where you spend most of your time, a term you need to know is FALL LINE," Jeff says. "The fall line is the gravity line an object would fall coming down the mountain. The fall line may or may not be in line with a trail or your desired path, but it is a line you must identify in order to learn balance and turning."

"I'm not sure I understand," Adam admits.

"Okay," Jeff says, "imagine dropping a ball from the top of the mountain. The ball has no idea which way the trail goes. It just rolls down the mountain according to the forces of gravity. That's the fall line. Unfortunately, the ball doesn't worry about trees, rocks, and other obstacles that might be in its path. It just falls. Riders don't have that luxury. We always have to be aware of the fall line because it's one of the factors we consider when making turns, carving, or traversing a slope."

"Traversing?" Adam asks.

"Yes. TRAVERSING a slope is when you place the board on edge and move across the slope rather than down the fall line. When you move from side to side in contrast to the fall line, that's called traversing the slope."

"So traversing is when you're moving on a line that's perpendicular to the fall line," Adam reviews.

"Right. You traverse at close to a ninety-degree angle to the fall line."

"Are there other terms I need to know?"

Jeff explains that up until now the discussion has focused on what are called groomed slopes: smoothly manicured surfaces. But there are many other kinds of surfaces Adam will likely encounter. "Sometimes we call perfectly groomed slopes CORDUROY," Jeff explains, "because the groomer will leave nice, straight, smooth lines in the snow just like a blanket of corduroy."

In addition to groomed, other types of surfaces can include:

THE PARK

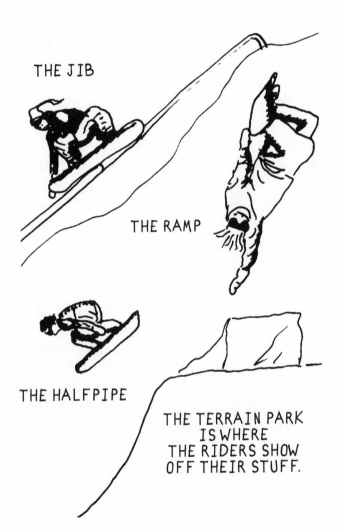

THE JIB

THE RAMP

THE HALFPIPE

THE TERRAIN PARK
IS WHERE
THE RIDERS SHOW
OFF THEIR STUFF.

- UNGROOMED snow, which is snow that's been untouched by grooming snowcats;
- SLUSH, which is a sloppy mixture of ice and snow;
- CRUD, which is an even sloppier mixture of melting snow and ice. Riding on crud is very difficult and requires some modifications in technique. Avoid it if you can;
- FRESH POWDER, which is one of the greatest surfaces for riding. It refers to freshly fallen, light, dry snow. It feels like soft baby powder and rides like a cushion. Again, riding powder requires some modifications in technique;
- PACKED POWDER, which is fresh powder that has been groomed;
- WINDBLOWN, which is fresh snow that has been densely packed by the wind. Windblown snow is often inconsistent and patchy; and
- MAN-MADE SNOW, which is a little harder and grainier than natural snow. When it's early or late in the season and nature isn't cooperating, man-made snow is a great alternative to no snow at all.

After he's finished writing, Adam looks back through his notes and observes, "You know, we still haven't answered my initial question."

"What was that?" Jeff asks.

"What are lifts?" Adam says.

Jeff gets his pencil back out and points to the trail map. "So far, we've talked about getting *down* the mountain. Lifts are the machines that get you *up* the mountain." Jeff proceeds to describe common types of lifts that a rider can use:

- CHAIR LIFT. As the name implies, it is a chair suspended on a cable. Riders wait in line as a continuous procession of chairs spaced fifty feet or so apart swing through a loading area, where the riders step forward, take a seat on the next moving chair, and get hoisted to the top of the slope. There's an art to loading and unloading on these lifts, which you will learn in your first lesson, but be aware that the chair lift isn't an amusement park ride: It doesn't stop just because you dropped a glove or because you aren't ready. You have to be ready to load and unload when it's your turn.

- GONDOLAS are enclosed cabins that hold between two and ten riders. Gondolas are usually reserved for longer runs. Some are even heated. Before you board a gondola, make sure it is going where you want to go. Otherwise, you might be in trouble for the trip down.

- A TRAM can hold up to one hundred people and their equipment, although the tram rides can sometimes last up to a half hour. Again, be sure the tram goes where you want to go.

- The ultimate lift is a HELICOPTER. Many resorts have limited-access areas that can only be accessed from heli-drops: That's when a helicopter lands on a plateau or peak and drops off the riders for some radical runs. Helicopter runs are sweet, but they can be dangerous. Make sure you map out your line before you go up, because once the chopper leaves, you're on your own.

TO THE TOP

THERE ARE MANY WAYS TO GET TO THE
TOP OF THE MOUNTAIN BUT ONLY ONE
WAY TO GET DOWN.

CHAIRLIFT

GONDOLA

TRAM

HELICOPTER

"I don't think I'll be taking any heli-drops for a while, although they sound cool!" Adam exclaims.

"They're great," Jeff says. "What you might want to do, if you decide to go OFF-PISTE, is hike into some moderate areas. Remember, snowboarding is an out-door adventure: Part of that adventure is trying new things, new areas, new runs. As long as you pay attention to where you're going, there's nothing wrong with venturing out beyond the boundaries."

"Off-piste?" Adam asks.

"Yes. That means going off the marked course or beyond the boundaries of the resort. PISTE is a French word for groomed, inbound trails. Off-piste, a term commonly used in North America, means 'off the main trails.' I'm sure you will try it before you know it."

"As long as I stay clear of the avalanches," Adam blurts out.

"Right," Jeff agrees, standing to indicate that this part of the lesson is over. "You know, I've been thinking about some of the other things you need to know," he adds. "There's a guy that owns a gym a couple of blocks from here I'd like you to meet."

"A gym?" Adam asks.

"Yeah. You look like you're in good shape, but there are some things I think you can do to get yourself ready for snowboarding. It's a different sport that uses different muscles."

Adam nods and affirms, "I'm not opposed to a good workout. Can we walk there from here?"

"Sure," Jeff says. "Let me get my coat."

EIGHT

BOARD SHAPE

It's a beautiful, crisp day. Jeff and Adam talk about different sports and various places they've been as they walk the two blocks to Palmer's Gym. When Adam enters the large white building, he spots a crowd of people to his right: An aerobics class is in session. When he turns to speak to Jeff, he sees that they have been joined by another man—a dark, stocky, athletic guy in his early thirties.

"Adam, this is Sean Palmer, the owner of the gym and one heck of a rider. Sean, this is our student, Adam."

The men shake hands and Sean says, "I understand that this is your first venture into snowboarding."

"That's right," Adam replies. "Before today, I knew absolutely nothing about it. I still don't know much, but I'm learning fast."

Jeff interjects, "Sean, I was hoping you could talk to Adam about a good workout routine. He's got a couple of weeks before he heads up to the mountain."

"Sure," Sean agrees. He then leads Adam to another room, this one full of free weights and lifting machines. "Have a seat," Sean says, pointing to one of the nearby benches. "So, do you think you're in pretty decent shape?"

"Yeah," Adam responds. "I run, swim, and skate. I played hockey in college, and I still get out on the ice occasionally, but it's strictly recreational now. No hard checks. I'd say I'm in better shape than most."

"You're probably right," Sean says. "But when it comes to riding a snowboard, you need to have a number of things going for you. You don't have to be a stud athlete to enjoy riding, and no matter what your level of conditioning, you can have a good time on the mountain. Being in good shape is just part of the equation. Good riding requires strength, stamina, flexibility, balance, and quick reflexes.

"No one of these is more important than the others. Snowboarding requires a little of everything, but that doesn't mean you have to be an Iron Man triathlete to ride. Most people, regardless of what kind of shape they're in, can have a good time riding with a little work and some preparation."

Adam takes out the notepad and starts writing.

"So, what should I do? Run?"

"Actually, running is a good cardiovascular exercise, but it's not an optimum workout for snowboarding. When working on cardiovascular conditioning (stamina) you need to make sure you perform exercises that will get your heart rate up between 60 and

90 percent of its maximum and keep it there for a minimum of twenty minutes."

"Whoa, how do I know my maximum heart rate?"

"That's easy. Subtract your age from 220 and that's what most physicians will call your maximum heart rate. A good workout will put your heart rate at over 60 but less than 90 percent of that maximum. Some appropriate exercises include cycling, swimming, aerobic training, in-line or ice skating, and basketball or racquetball. As long as you perform these activities regularly and make sure you work out for at least twenty to thirty minutes, you will see your cardiovascular stamina improve."

Adam knows he's in good shape, but he's never considered his maximum heart rate or the length of time he works out. "Are there other exercises I need to do for strength, balance, and the flexibility?"

"Yes," Sean says. "Not only will you need to consider other exercises, first and foremost you need to do an honest assessment of your current fitness. Are you strong for your age and size? Do you tire easily, or do you have better-than-average stamina? How flexible are you, really? How would you rate your balance, coordination, and reflexes compared not only to other men your age, but also relative to your own strength and stamina?

"Like most people, you will be weak in some areas and strong in others. Focus on your weak areas and strike a balance with your strong areas. Assume for a moment that your cardiovascular stamina is good, but you need to work on your strength and flexibility. Tailor your workouts so you're focusing, say, 80 percent of your efforts on strength and flexibility and 20 percent on balance and stamina. If you have great strength and great balance but tire too easily, you should spend the majority of your workout time on endurance. Be honest with yourself."

Sean tells Adam that a full range of strengthening exercises is necessary to prepare for snowboarding. "Don't just assume that it's all lower body," he cautions. "When it comes to riding, your abdominals, arms, and back muscles are just as important as your legs. Work on everything. Lift weights and get involved in a training program at a local gym. If that's not feasible, then set aside at least fifteen to thirty minutes at home to perform some key exercises."

Some of the exercises Sean outlines include:

- Push-ups, which work on the triceps, quadriceps, pectorals, and lateral oblique muscles of the upper body;
- Sit-ups, which work on strengthening the abdominal muscles. Be sure to keep your knees bent, and try to keep your hands closed behind your head. This will help reduce the potential for back problems.
- Triceps lifts, where, from a seated position, you place your hands on the floor in back and perform what resemble backward push-ups. This isolates the triceps and quadriceps and builds greater strength in the upper arms.
- Frontside leg lifts, where you get on your hands

and knees and slowly lift one knee up toward
the chest. Then extend that leg fully without
letting it touch the floor. Repeat with both legs
for as many repetitions as possible;

- Backside leg lifts, where you rest on your back
  and slowly lift one leg, keeping the leg as
  straight as possible, until it extends straight up.
  Next, lower the leg as slowly as possible. Repeat
  with the other leg. Perform as many repetitions
  as possible.

- Side leg lifts, where you lie on your side and
  raise one leg, then the other. This works the
  thighs and abdominal muscles.

- Squats, for which you bend your knees and
  squat into a sitting position, then stand erect, all
  the while keeping your back straight.

- Calf raises, where you stand on a stair or slightly
  elevated platform with your heels extended off
  the edge. By repeatedly moving from the toes
  to a position where the heels hang over the
  edge, you develop strength and resilience in the
  calf muscles.

- Kneel lunges, for which you take one long
  stride forward and stop, then slowly lower yourself onto your back knee, while keeping your
  head up and back straight. This strengthens the
  entire lower body while also helping you learn
  balance.

- Wall sits, for which you sit in an imaginary
  chair with your back against a wall. This exercise strengthens the thigh and hamstring

muscles and simulates the pressure that is likely to be placed on your knees.

"All these exercises require dedication and consistency," Sean explains. "Don't think you can work out once or twice and be ready. Dedicate fifteen to thirty minutes every day to your workout. Make sure you do the exercises correctly so that you work the muscles you're trying to strengthen."

Some keys to remember are:

- Always breathe while exercising. Fill your lungs while going through the repetitions. That way, your muscles will work better, you will feel better, and you will get a better overall workout.

- Concentrate on the muscle group being worked. It's easy to get lazy and let other muscles do the work for the weaker muscle groups. By staying focused on what muscles are being exercised, you get more out of the exercise and reduce the risk of injury.

- Use proper technique when exercising, and take it slow. By slowly working through the repetitions, you let kinetic energy and the laws of physics work *for* you. If you have to do fewer reps in order to do the exercise correctly, so be it. It's more important to use good form than it is to do lots of reps poorly.

- Don't overdo it. Work hard but smart. It doesn't do you any good to work beyond your limits and strain a muscle. If you continue to work out every day, you will see gradual but consistent improvement. There's no reason to overdo it.

Adam writes all of this down. "I assume I need to work on flexibility at the same time I'm working on strength, right?"

"You got it," Sean acknowledges. "Remember, no aspect of your conditioning is more or less important than any other. You need to incorporate a full range of stretching exercises with your strength and stamina training."

Sean then demonstrates several stretching exercises:

- Toe touches. Bend from the waist and touch your toes.
- Thigh pulls. Stand on one foot and grab the other foot behind you, pulling the foot and leg up so that the upper thigh muscle is stretched.
- Calf leans. Stand three or four feet away from a wall, then slowly lean into the wall, keeping your heels on the floor. This stretches the calf and lower leg muscles.
- Back arch. Lie on your stomach and lift your head, shoulders, and legs so that the back is arched and the abdominal muscles are stretched.
- Torso twist. While sitting in a chair or standing with feet apart, twist your torso from side to side, then lean from side to side. This stretches the back, shoulders, and abdominals.
- Behind-the-back pull. Clasp your hands together behind your back, and stretch your arms as far away from your body as possible. This stretches the shoulders and arms.

"Again, it's important that you breathe during these stretching exercises, and make darned sure you use good form," Sean advises. "The objective is to get in good shape without hurting yourself."

"What about balance and reflexes?" Adam asks.

Sean answers by saying how a lot of these exercises will improve Adam's balance, although there are some specific drills he can do to better prepare himself for his first day out on the snow:

- Stand on a narrow board with your feet positioned as they will be on your snowboard. While you won't get the same feel as you will when going down a slope, this will prepare you for the kind of balancing maneuvers you will experience when riding.

- Try skateboarding. The carryovers from skateboarding to snowboarding are numerous. Once you've perfected the balance and poise necessary to skateboard, the transition to a snowboard will be a lot easier.

- Spend time in your boots and bindings before going onto the slopes. Practice tilting the board on edge in your living room. While it will be very different out on the mountain, getting comfortable with your equipment and the movements will do nothing but help.

"As for your reflexes," Sean adds, "all you can do is sharpen your natural quickness. Basketball and other reaction sports will go a long way toward improving your reflexes and sharpening your concentration. Remember, snowboarding is not a static sport. You have to react to your environment and your equipment. These drills will help you learn by

BETTER CONDITIONING LEADS TO BETTER RIDING.

SWIMMING

RUNNING

CYCLING

keeping your fatigue factor down. If you follow this workout, you can prepare your body for the new experience of riding."

"Anything else?" Adam asks.

"Yes. You haven't lived here very long, have you?"

"No," Adam admits. "In fact, I'm very new to the area."

"Have you ever experienced altitude sickness?"

"What's that?"

"Because air is thinner at higher altitudes, many people experience what's known as ALTITUDE SICKNESS. At higher altitudes the body must work harder to get enough oxygen to the brain. This can cause dizziness, fatigue, nausea, blurred vision, and impaired judgment. Be aware of this potential danger, and give yourself plenty of time to adjust to your new environment. Don't expect to do the same things you can do at sea level. After a few hours or maybe a couple of days, your body will adjust to the altitude and you'll be fine. In the meantime, drink plenty of water and take long, deep breaths. Which brings up another point."

"What's that?" Adam asks.

"Don't drink alcohol or caffeine. Your body is bound to become dehydrated during your first few runs. Caffeine and alcohol are diuretics that actually reduce the amount of fluids in your body. Alcohol also slows your reflexes and impairs your judgment. Stick to water. Even sodas don't replenish your fluids like water. Remember, this is an active sport just like tennis, basketball, or hockey. You wouldn't drink alcohol while playing those sports. Snowboarding is no different."

"Point taken," Adam states as he looks back through his notes. Sean interrupts him with a question.

"Has anyone explained the responsibility code to you? It's like a code of ethics and safety for all riders."

"No."

"It's very important," Sean continues. "There are certain essentials of etiquette and safety everyone needs to know before setting foot on the snow. If you have time, I'd be happy to go over them with you."

"Sure," Adam says. "I might not be good, but I want to follow the rules."

Nine

Freestyle Courtesy

Sean grabs a bottle of water from a nearby cooler and offers one to Adam, who gladly accepts. "You know, snowboarding hasn't always had the best reputation," Sean resumes.

"I know," Adam responds. "Jeff said that for a while mountains actually banned riders."

Sean nods. "Snowboarding was seen as a radical snow-surfing distraction to real skiers, and riders were considered uncontrollable renegades who had no business being on the mountain. Fortunately, that attitude has changed. However, it's important that you understand the rules of riding. Anyone who rides irresponsibly is a bad reflection on all of us."

"I know what you mean," Adam says. "People think I'm a lunatic because I jump out of airplanes."

Sean smiles and nods. "Okay," he proceeds, "the first thing to remember is that you are not the only person on the mountain. There will be other riders and skiers out there with you, some better than you and some not as good. It's like driving down an un-marked highway with driving-school students and NASCAR drivers all around you. Be alert.

"Always be considerate of those around you. The number-one rule in riding is the golden rule: Do unto others as you would have them do unto you."

"Good advice," Adam says, while writing.

Sean goes on to explain that there are some pre-cautionary measures all riders need to take to ensure their safety and the safety of those around them.

- First, riders need to check their equipment and make sure bindings are secured before going onto the slopes. Unlike skis, snowboard bind-ings do not release when the rider falls, and boards do not have brakes. Because of that, it's imperative that riders stay on their boards. Never detach both boots from your bindings when you're on the slopes. A freefalling snow-board is a dangerous projectile that can maim or even kill someone.
- Stretch and go through some warm-up exer-cises before going out on the mountain. The more physically prepared you are for your ride, the more fun it will be. You also lower your risk of pulling a muscle or otherwise injuring your-self when you properly warm up. Don't strap on a snowboard before preparing your body.
- Quit before you become too tired. Most acci-dents happen when you've stayed out on the mountain one run too long. When you become fatigued, stop, rest, and drink some water—get

your strength and concentration back—before going back out.

- Be aware of the weather conditions before you venture out onto the mountain. It might be a beautiful day at the base, but a storm could be brewing in the vicinity. Conditions sometimes worsen so quickly that you can experience a WHITEOUT. That's when heavy snow and strong winds reduce visibility to near zero. When that happens, stop and move to a secure area on a side of the slope. Either wait for the storm to pass or slowly traverse the hill, staying near the side of the slope.

"No one expects you to be an expert meteorologist," Sean concedes. "Check the ski patrol report before going out on your first run. It should give you the projected weather conditions as well as snow conditions and potential avalanche sites."

Adam is suddenly lost. He asks, "What's a SKI PATROL?"

"They are the rescue squad, the highway patrol, the paramedics, and the traffic cops all rolled into one. They set up the ski area at the beginning of each day, check dangerous areas, and sometimes trigger avalanches to get them out of the way when no one's around. The ski patrol also acts as a rescue team out on the mountain, administering first aid and carefully getting the injured rider down. When you show up for your first day, you need to identify the ski patrol, and keep an eye out for them throughout the day."

"Good idea," Adam says. It hadn't occurred to him until now that someone might have to carry him off the mountain if he were to injure himself.

"Now these safety tips are important," Sean adds, "but nothing is more important than your adherence to the responsibility code. This is a universally accepted code of behavior for all ski and snowboard areas. A lot of it is common sense, but none of it should be taken for granted."

That said, Sean goes on to explain the code:

- *Ride in control.* In order to improve, a rider is going to have to push the limits of his or her ability but should never push to the point of riding out of control. Always be able to stop, and always ride in a way so as to avoid other people or objects. In people's zeal to try new things, they often forget that there are others around them who might not appreciate their antics.

- *People below you on the slope always have the right of way.* It's your responsibility to avoid them. If people in front of you are looking where they're going, they can't very well check behind them. Be aware of a rider's blind side. Obviously, a rider's backside, or heelside, is his or her blind side. No one has eyes in the back of his or her head, so when riders make a heel-edge turn, they are turning to a blind side. If you're coming up behind that rider, it's your responsibility to give him or her a wide berth.

- *Never stop in a tight area or an area where people above you cannot see you.* That's a little like saying,

"Don't wander out into the middle of a freeway at night." It's amazing how many people stop in blind spots and then wonder why people above them don't see them. If you must stop, move to the side of the slope and position yourself where you aren't an obstacle. Once you stop, it's your responsibility to be out of the way.

- *Whenever starting from a dead stop or merging onto another trail, look uphill to make sure you aren't cutting in front of someone.* If you're jumping out into the flow of traffic, you need to make sure someone isn't bearing down on you from above.

- *If you're hiking uphill, be sure you move to the side of the slope* so as not to disrupt other riders. Nothing is wrong with wanting to go back uphill to take a jump or make a turn again. If you do, make sure you move to the side.

- *Always use a safety device such as a safety line or ankle harness* so that the board won't get away from you if and when you remove it while on the mountain. Stay with your equipment at all times.

- *Obey all signs and warnings.* If the ski patrol has closed an area, it's for a good reason. Keep off closed trails and stay away from dangerous areas. You don't need to add to the sport's inherent dangers by being an idiot.

- *Make sure you know how to load, unload, and ride a lift before stepping into line.* There are safety factors as well as courtesy factors in proper lift etiquette.

> One of the first things your instructor will teach
> you is how to get on and off a lift. Pay attention.
> It's important.
>
> - If you come across an injured person, stop, eval-
>   uate the situation, administer first aid if you are
>   qualified, and wait for the ski patrol.

Adam looks up when he realizes Sean has
stopped. "Is that it?" he asks.

"That's it," Sean states. "As I told you, most of it is
common sense. Hey, you know, I've got something
else that might help you."

Sean leads Adam down a hallway and into the ad-
ministrative areas of the gym, where he goes over to a
file cabinet and starts flipping through some files.
"I've kept this old thing here knowing that someday,
someone would need it. I guess that day has come."
He looks a moment longer, then says, "Aha, here it
is." Sean pulls out a small book and hands it to Adam.

"What is it?"

"A glossary of snowboard terms," Sean says.
"We've always been accused of having our own language, so a while back I wrote down some of the
terms unique to snowboarding. I haven't used it in
some time, but maybe you can."

"I'm sure I can," Adam affirms. "Thanks for everything, Sean. This has been great."

"No worries," Sean concludes. "You'll be railing
down some sick runs before you know it."

With that, Adam says good-bye and steps out into
his brave new world.

GOLDEN RULE

ALWAYS USE THE GOLDEN RULE WHEN RIDING. BE MINDFUL OF OTHERS AND KNOW THE RESPONSIBILITY CODE.

Ten

Cutting-Edge Ending

A month later Adam is back at his office, arranging the documents in his in-box and checking his voice mail before making his morning trek to the coffee machine. When he arrives at the break room, Chris and Leta are standing near the door.

"Hey, Adam, how's that new board working out?" Chris asks.

"It's great," Adam declares. "I've opened up a little more with it, and it took a few runs to get the bindings set; but now that I'm dialed in, it's sweet. I'm riding again this weekend, if you want to come."

"Sure," Chris agrees, amazed by how much Adam has learned in the last few weeks. The guy is obviously an athlete, but Chris has never seen progress like this from anyone else.

Like most people, Adam had spent much of the first day on his back on the bunny slopes, but within a day and a half he was linking turns, carving smooth edges, and moving to some of the more challenging intermediate slopes. Now, just a few weeks later, Adam is a terrain park wizard. He's already tried the half pipe, and hiked into some off-piste areas for some spectacular jumps.

At this rate, Chris figures, this guy will be world-class in a year or less. In the meantime, he has a new friend, and as far as Chris can tell, Adam seems a lot happier. "Why don't I come by your place on Saturday morning?" he suggests.

"Better make it Sunday, as I've already made plans for Saturday," Adam says, smiling as he and Leta steal guilty glances at each other.

"What's up with you two anyway?" Chris asks his two office friends.

"Nothing. I've got to get back to work," Leta declares, sharing another momentary glance with Adam before she excuses herself and heads back toward her office.

Adam turns to Chris but doesn't lose the smile. "I'll see you around noon on Sunday," he says, then he, too, heads back down the hallway.

"See you Sunday," Chris affirms, while swirling a cup of coffee and staring after his friends. Office life is getting more interesting by the day.

ELEVEN

PALMER'S GLOSSARY

aerials. Maneuvers or tricks performed while in the air. A competitive form of riding.

air, or **catch air.** To jump or become airborne on a snowboard.

alpine carving. *See* **carve.**

altitude sickness. The body's adverse reaction to dramatic changes in elevation, caused by the oxygen variance between altitudes. Symptoms include dizziness, nausea, fatigue, blurred vision, and impaired judgment.

artificial snow. Man-made snow crystals created by blasting a fine spray of water into cold air. Artificial snow is heavier and icier than natural snow.

avalanche. A snowslide in which large sections of snow become dislodged and slide down the mountain. A very dangerous and potentially deadly situation.

back foot. The foot closest to the tail of the board—
the right foot for regular riders and the left foot
for goofy riders.

backside, or **backside turn.** The side behind the
rider, or a turn to the heelside edge of the board.

bail. (1) The clip on a hard-boot, plate-binding
system. (2) A complete surrender during the
middle of a maneuver where the rider "bails
out" and falls.

base. (1) The bottom of the mountain where the
lodge is located. (2) The average depth of snow
covering the mountain. (3) The bottom or under-
side of the board.

base lodge. The building at the base of the mountain that usually houses instructors' offices, a
restaurant, lockers and locker rooms, and a shop
filled with equipment and apparel.

big air. Large jumps.

bindings. The mechanism that holds a rider's boots
to the board. The most important piece of equipment in riding.

black diamond. The designation for advanced runs.

blue square. The designation for intermediate runs.

board. A snowboard.

boardercross. Multiple riders (usually, a group of
six) simultaneously racing down a pre-set terrain
course to the finish line. The first rider across the
line wins.

bomb hole, or **hole.** The indentation left in the landing zone of a jump or drop.

bone. A straightened leg while performing a jump.

bonk. To bounce off objects while descending the slope.

bumps. *See* **moguls.**

bunny slope. The most gentle slope on the mountain, usually set aside for beginners.

camber. The arch or bow in the board that absorbs the weight of the rider and distributes it throughout the board.

Canadian bacon. One of many grabs performed during aerial maneuvers. These grabs are collectively known as food tricks.

carve. A smooth turn on the edge of a snowboard.

carving board. One of four different types of snowboards designed for speed and clean turning. Not designed for tricks, jumps, or terrain park maneuvers.

cat tracks. Narrow trails for beginner access that traverse down steep areas.

catching air. *See* **air.**

catching an edge. An accident where the edge of the board digs into an unseen rut or chunk of ice and causes the rider to fall.

chair lift. The most common type of lift up the hill, where the rider loads onto a chair suspended by a cable that hoists him or her up to the top of the slope.

chatter. The vibration experienced when a snow-board skips out, catching and releasing its edge.

code, or **responsibility code.** The international rules of behavior and conduct when riding or skiing.

coin-operated course. A slalom course where, for a nominal fee, amateur riders can time their runs.

control gate, or **gate.** A pole, or set of poles, placed at intervals along a slope, thus establishing the boundaries for the course. Racers must race around or through the control gates.

corduroy. Well-groomed snow with fresh, straight grooming lines still intact. The snow, when groomed in this fashion, looks like a blanket of corduroy.

cornice. An overhanging ridge of snow.

couloir, or **chute.** A steep gully of snow on the side of a mountain.

crud. A slushy mixture of snow and ice that is very difficult to maneuver in and very unpleasant for the rider.

crust. A hard surface of snow covering a soft under-layer. Crusts form through the thawing and re-freezing of the top layer of snow.

derby. A race on an unprepared mountain that is simply a top-to-bottom race. Racers pick their own lines and get from top to bottom as fast as they can.

double black diamond. The designation for the most difficult, expert runs.

drop. Air caught from riding off vertical features such as cliffs and rocks.

dual-lens goggles. Goggles with two pairs of lenses separated by air and ventilated to reduce fogging.

dual slalom. A head-to-head race on two identical, parallel slalom courses.

duck. A stance where the back foot is turned toward the tail of the board while the front foot is turned toward the nose.

edge. The corner of the board where the base meets the sidewall at a narrow strip of stainless steel.

effective edge. The amount of board edge in contact with the snow during a turn. Race and carving boards have greater effective edges than do freeride and freestyle boards.

endo. A very bad wipeout, where the rider tumbles end over end down the mountain.

Eurocarve. Turning with an exaggerated body lean so that the body often drags in the snow.

face. The steep side of a mountain.

face plant. Falling on your face.

fakie. Riding tail first or doing tricks where the takeoff or landing is performed tail first.

fall line. The gravity line, or the line a ball would take if rolled down a slope. Finding the fall line is critical to maintaining balance and control on the slopes.

fanny pack. A small pouch worn around the waist.

flatbottom. Hitting a flat surface after making a jump. A jarring and often dangerous maneuver.

flex. The degree to which a board bends under pressure.

food trick. Grabbing the edge of the board during an aerial maneuver.

freeride. (1) A style of riding that embodies certain elements of freestyle trick riding and carving or racing. Freeriding is the most common style of snowboarding. (2) One of four types of snowboards. Freeride boards are designed for freeride-style riding.

freestyle. (1) A style of riding most often characterized by aerials, jumps, jibs, bonks, and other tricks. Freestyle riding puts more emphasis on style and execution than speed and turning. (2) One of four types of snowboards. Freestyle boards are designed for freestyle riding.

fresh powder. Newly fallen, light, dry snow that has been untouched by grooming machines.

frontside, or **frontside turn.** The side in front of the rider, or a turn to the toeside edge of the board.

frostbite. A serious medical condition in which the cell tissue of the extremities freezes.

garland. Linked turns across a fall line.

gates, or **racing gates.** Flags, or poles, placed in the snow around which racers must maneuver. Spacing between gates dictates the type of race being run.

giant slalom. A slalom race where the gates are farther apart (fifteen to twenty-three meters) than a standard slalom course, placing greater emphasis on speed and technique.

glide. Sliding downhill without using the board's edges.

gnarly. (1) Very difficult, (2) impressive, or (3) rough or "gnarled."

goggles. Protective eyewear that should be worn by all snowboard riders.

gondola. An enclosed lift used to transport two or more riders up long distances. Gondolas are often heated.

goofy. A stance where the rider places his or her right foot forward on the board.

goofy test. A test to determine whether a rider is regular or goofy-footed. The rider runs and imagines he or she is stopping on a sheet of ice. If the rider stops right-foot-forward, the rider is goofy. If the rider stops left-foot-forward, the rider is regular or straight-footed.

green circle. The designation for beginner slopes.

groomed. Trails or runs that have been smoothed by snowcats or grooming machines prior to a day of riding.

group lesson. An instructional session in which the student-to-instructor ratio is two or more to one.

half pipe. A manufactured gully in the snow that resembles the bottom half of a large culvert pipe. Riders perform tricks by riding up the sides of the half pipe and becoming airborne.

hard boot. A boot made of hard, rigid plastic that restricts ankle movement. Hard boots are worn primarily by racers and carving riders. Hard boots originated from mountaineering boots.

hardpack. Crusty, packed snow.

heel edge. The edge of the board on the rider's back or heelside.

heel turn. A turn in the direction of the rider's back or heelside. The heelside turn is a blind turn that should be performed with caution.

heelside. The backside edge of the board closest to the rider's heels.

helicopter. A flying machine used by riders to reach off-piste or extreme areas—the ultimate snowboard lift.

heli-drop. Transportation to an otherwise inaccessible area of a mountain by helicopter and getting dropped off for a run.

high-back binding. A soft-boot binding system where straps hold the toe and ankle of the boot, and the back is supported by a long plastic strip that extends up the back of the rider's leg.

hit. The launch point in the half pipe or any jump.

hypothermia. A dangerous medical condition where a rider's core body temperature is reduced as a result of exposure to extreme cold.

invert. Any aerial trick where the rider is upside down.

jacket. One piece of outerwear for snowboarding.

jibbing. The act of hitting or sliding along anything artificial set within the confines of the terrain park or other areas.

jump. An airborne maneuver.

lead hand, or **lead foot.** The hand or foot closest to the front of the board.

lift. (1) Any of a number of machines used to transport riders up the slopes. (2) A canting wedge used to lift the rider's toe or heel.

lift line. The orderly line of riders waiting to load onto a lift.

lift ticket. Tickets, often laminated and attached with hooks, which act as the rider's pass to use the mountain. Lift tickets can be bought daily, weekly, or seasonally.

linking. Connecting a series of turns together without stopping or falling.

line. A rider's intended path down the mountain.

liner. A soft material inside a hard snowboard boot that separates and cushions the rider's foot from the shell of the hard boot.

lip. The top of a jump or the top edge of a half pipe.

loading. The act of getting onto a lift.

man-made snow. Artificial snow created by pumping a fine spray of water at high pressure into the cold air. Artificial snow packs harder than natural snow, but when the weather does not cooperate, it beats having no snow at all.

moguls. From the Alps colloquialism *mugel,* which means "small mound." These mounds are formed when many riders turn along the same path.

nose. Front portion of the snowboard.

nose grabs. A snowboard trick where the rider catches air and grabs the front of his or her board.

nosebone. A jump where the rider's front leg is straight and the back leg is flexed.

obstacles. Man-made objects such as picnic tables, cars, and handrails placed in the terrain park so riders can do tricks on, over, or around them.

off-piste. An ungroomed slope.

ollie. Catching air with a board without going off a jump. The maneuver is achieved by stepping on the tail of the board while pulling up on the nose of the board.

pack. To hit hard.

packed powder. Freshly groomed, soft, dry snow.

piste. A groomed trail.

pit-zips. A unique zipper system in snowboarding jackets that ventilate the rider's underarms.

plate binding. A hard-boot binding system used by many carving and racing riders.

powder. Fresh, light, dry snow that resembles baby powder.

private lesson. An instructional session in which the student-to-teacher ratio is one to one.

P-tex. A plastic material used to repair abrasions on the base of a snowboard.

race board. The longest and stiffest of the four types of snowboards, designed specifically for racing.

rad. Short for *radical,* a common colloquialism for something extreme.

rail. (1) A wooden structure embedded in a half pipe, (2) to ride hard and well, or (3) to make a completely carved turn without displacement or edge washout.

rail slide. Sliding along a rail.

recyclers. Snowboards made out of recycled snowboards or skis.

regular. A stance where the left foot is forward on the snowboard.

riding. The proper term for snowboarding.

roll-out deck. (1) The exit area of the half pipe. (2) Platforms along either side of the half pipe at the same level as the lip.

run. A trail or slope.

runout. The flat area at the base of a run.

shell. Outer portion of the boot.

shell binding. A soft-boot binding system that looks like a hard plastic sandal attached to the board. The shell binding has a moderately high plastic back and straps that hold the toe of the boot in place.

shred. Fast, stylish riding.

Shred Betty. A politically incorrect colloquialism for a female snowboarder.

sick run. An extremely intense slope.

sidecut. The curvature which makes the waist of the board narrower than the nose and tail and gives the board an hourglass shape.

sideslip. A sideways slide down a slope, not on edge.

sidewall. The side of the snowboard.

ski patrol. Specially trained personnel who set up the mountain each day and act as the rescue squad; the ski police.

sky-back. Systems with plastic back extending up to the rider's calf muscle.

slalom. A race through a series of gates set close together (eight to twelve meters apart) down a slope. Racers must maneuver around or between the gates as quickly and efficiently as possible.

slam. Crash.

slopestyle. One of many freestyle competitions judged on style, transition, rotation, and landing.

sluff. A mini-avalanche created when a rider displaces snow on a steep slope by continuous carving.

slush. An unpleasant combination of melting snow and ice.

snow blindness. A serious medical condition where the cornea of the eye is burned due to exposure to sunlight reflected off bright snow.

snowboard pants. Generally baggy pants with added padding.

snowgun. The device that is used to spray man-made snow out onto a slope.

snurfer. The first snowboard, invented by Sherman Poppen.

soft boot. A semiflexible snowboarding boot that resembles a hard hiking boot or a standard-issue combat boot. Soft boots require soft-boot bindings and are the preferred choice of most nonracers.

spins. Airborne tricks where the rider rotates. Spins usually are defined by the degrees of rotation(s). A 180 is a half rotation, a 360 one full rotation, and a 720 two full rotations on one jump.

stale fish. A grab during a jump where the rider grabs the backside edge of the board between the bindings.

step-in bindings. A boot-binding system, where the rider simply steps into the binding to secure the connection.

stiffy. A jump where both the rider's legs are straightened.

stinky, or **stinkbug.** A wider-than-average stance.

sunglasses. A form of protective eyewear that prevents serious eye damage by protecting the eyes from excessive ultraviolet rays.

super G. A race in which the gates are very far apart (twenty-five to thirty-nine meters) and speed is at a premium.

switch–stance. *See* **fakie.**

table tops. Flat surfaces in between the takeoff and landing of a jump.

tail. The back portion of the board.

tail grabs. Airborne tricks in which the rider grabs the rear of his or her board.

terrain park. A specific area designated for freestyle riding. Obstacles and jumps are set up in the terrain park so that riders can jib, jump, and bonk in a predetermined area. The half pipe is usually in, or adjacent to, the terrain park.

toe edge, or **toe turn.** The edge of the board on the rider's front or toe side.

trail. A slope or run.

trail map. A map outlining a snowboard mountain and the various difficulties of each of the trails.

tram. Large enclosed cabin that can accommodate up to one hundred riders and equipment while transporting them to the top of the slope. Usually reserved for long runs or bottom-to-top transit.

traverse. Maneuvering across the slope at close to a perpendicular angle to the fall line.

tree line. The altitude at which trees stop growing.

tree well. The displacement of snow in which a tree sits.

tuning center. The area of the snowboard shop devoted to tuning and repairing boards.

turn. A motion where the snowboard and rider change directions.

tweak. A maneuver where the board is pulled either forward or backward during a jump.

ungroomed. Trails that have been left untouched by grooming machines.

unloading. The act (or art) of getting off a lift at the top of the mountain.

waist. The center of the board, designed to be narrower than the nose and the tail.

waist pack, or **fanny pack.** A small pouch accessory that can be carried around the rider's waist. It holds valuables, food, and other items the rider deems essential for mountain use.

whiteout. Zero-visibility conditions experienced during heavy snow and wind.

wicket. A hook that attaches to the rider's jacket or pants on which an adhesive lift ticket is mounted.

wicking. A characteristic of clothing in which moisture is absorbed by the clothes and moved away from the weaver.

windblown. Fresh snow that has been densely packed by the wind.

windchill factor. A meteorological calculation designed to show how cold the combined wind and temperature feel against the skin.

wipeout. A fall.

World Extreme Championship. The ultimate freestyle competition in which racers pick the sickest runs down the toughest mountains and try to make it down without killing themselves.